EVERY CHRISTIAN
A SOUL WINNER

EVERY CHRISTIAN
A SOUL WINNER

---

by

STANLEY TAM

as
told
to

KEN ANDERSON

THOMAS NELSON PUBLISHERS
Nashville • Camden • New York

Published in Nashville, Tennessee, by Thomas Nelson, Inc. and distributed in Canada by Lawson Falle, Ltd., Cambridge, Ontario.

Printed in the United States of America.

Library of Congress Cataloging in Publication Data
Tam, Stanley, 1915-
    Every Christian a soul winner.
    1. Evangelistic work.   2. Witness bearing (Christianity) I.
Anderson, Kenneth, 1917-   II. Title.
BV3790.T25   248'.5   75-17771
ISBN 0-8407-5093-5

Soul winning is the greatest business in the world, and I doubt if God has for us a more glorious work in heaven. Think of the priceless value of a soul. It was one of the greatest days of my life when I met Ken Anderson in 1960, a man thoroughly dedicated to this ministry. He has been a constant encouragement to me. I will ever be grateful to him for his willingness to use his great skill in putting my experiences into readable print.

R. STANLEY TAM

CONTENTS

CHAPTER ONE

SOUL WINNERS WHO DON'T WIN SOULS

No subject lists higher on the agenda of Mr. Average Evangelical than soul winning.

On the radio, from the pulpit, in Sunday school classes, evangelicals stress the need for reaching out to the lost. You can buy shelves of books on the subject. Some excellent audio visual aids have been produced.

Each year, I travel the full girth of North America, speaking in churches, to layman's groups, at conferences, in college chapels. No need to announce the topic when I come. People know Stanley Tam will talk to them about soul winning.

And it heartens me to see the enthusiasm with which Christians respond to the subject.

Respond to the subject, I say.

Yes, to the "subject." But unfortunately—I should perhaps say tragically—not always to the "project" itself.

Ad libs from people in attendance at my meetings run something like this.

9

"You really put it right on the line, Mr. Tam."

"It's my daily prayer, to be an effective soul winner."

"I want this more than anything else in my Christian life."

"But . . ."

That little three letter conjunction "but," I'm sorry to say, tends to characterize the performance record of most Christians I meet.

They know they should.

They want to.

They hope to.

The high majority intend to.

But they don't.

Statistics tend to be cold and uninteresting. In the case of Christians and this business of personal soul winning, statistics unearth some cold, hard facts. Namely that, according to survey's made among evangelicals, ninety six percent have never led a soul to Christ.

Maybe you are part of that statistic!

"I want with all my heart to be a soul winner," you say. "I hear other Christians talk about the joy of leading people to Christ. I want to experience that joy for myself, more than anything I know, but it just doesn't happen."

Well, I have some startling and encouraging news for you.

If you are a Christian, one who has been brought from the darkness of sin into the liberating light of transformation through faith in Jesus Christ, you are already a soul winner!

Sounds like I've dialed the wrong number?

10

Not at all!

My contention is as Scriptural as John 3:16. For all your timidity, your reluctance, your excuses, whatever, you are a soul winner right now. Just as sure as D. L. Moody was. Or Billy Sunday. Or any present day Christian active in bringing men to Christ.

Oh, you may not be a functioning soul winner. That's the other side of the coin. But you *are* a soul winner none-the-less.

Let me clarify.

When one has been genuinely born anew, God tells us, *His Spirit beareth witness with our spirit, that we are the children of God.*[1] Further, He tells us we are to *walk not after the flesh but after the Spirit.*[2] And that we are to be *filled with the Spirit.*[3] All of which adds up to the fantastic question: *What? Know ye not that your body is the temple of the Holy Spirit, who is in you, whom ye have of God, and ye are not your own?*[4]

Ye were sealed with that Holy Spirit of promise,[5] the Bible verifies. The word "sealed" speaks of a mark of identification, a mark of genuineness—God's "Good Housekeeping Seal of Approval," you might say.

Continuing, concerning this fantastic truth of the Holy Spirit being within you, we are told, *Who is the earnest of our inheritance until the redemption of the purchased possession, unto the praise of His glory.*[6]

"Earnest" here speaks of what we might call a down payment. At the moment of your conversion, the Holy Spirit enters your life. He is proof positive that you have been transformed from a child of Satan into a child of God!

We have a lot of emphasis today on physical manifestations of the Holy Spirit. Without these, some insist, you can't really know whether or not you are a Christian. Concerning the testimony of the Lord Jesus through His life here on earth, however, the Bible says: *These are written, that ye might believe that Jesus is the Christ, the Son of God; and that believing ye might have life through His name.*[7]

The Holy Spirit within you verifies this life, as attested in the Word of God.

Now it is wonderful to "feel" like a Christian. *If any man be in Christ,* the Bible assures us, *he is a new creation.*[8] David sang: *Thou wilt show me the path of life. In Thy presence is fullness of joy; at thy right hand there are pleasures for evermore.*[9]

Yes, the Christian life is meant to be a joyful, spiritually productive experience. But the Bible also speaks of unproductive Christians who shall *be saved, yet as by fire.*[10]

The clarity with which the Bible speaks about our purpose, our privileges, as human beings staggers me. I can't see how anyone, if he'll read the Bible, can miss the point. We aren't a mass of genetic accidents milling across the face of the earth but creatures purposefully designed to fulfill a destiny of eternal significance.

Now please read carefully.

The reason I say that, if you are a Christian, you are already a soul winner is very simple. The Holy Spirit—not you or any other human being on earth —is the only one who can bring men to Christ. He

—the Holy Spirit—is the soul winner, and He—the Holy Spirit—indwells every Christian.

If, then, you are to have the joy of seeing men won to Christ, it cannot be through your own effort. It must happen through the outflow of the Holy Spirit from your life.

Do the work of an evangelist, the Apostle exhorted Timothy. *Make full proof of thy ministry.*[11] In those days, Christians hadn't been categorized into "laymen" and "full time" as we do today. There were no colleges, no seminaries.

I don't oppose Christian training, mind you. If you've read the book *God Owns My Business,* you know something of the stewardship effort extended by our business. Prime target for our stewardship happens to be the training of national Christians for work as pastors, teachers and evangelists.

The only point I'm trying to get across is that Paul and his protege Timothy classified as laity.

Now, of course, proper training can be very helpful to the soul winner. As stated a few paragraphs back, I devote most of my weekends each year to conducting seminars on the subject, trying to help other laymen come to grips with their responsibility and opportunity as children of God.

We discuss methodology at these seminars. Just as successful salesmanship involves tested techniques, a working knowledge of human motivations, so also does personal evangelism.

But you can have a house all wired up like a Christmas tree. Unless the switch is on to the power station, however, you could just as well be living in a cave.

So with the Christian.

We have seen that the Holy Spirit indwells the Christian.

He indwells you!

Then why are you not winning souls to Christ? The answer is that you have the Holy Spirit but He doesn't have you.

Paradoxical as it may seem, you are a soul winner who isn't winning souls! A potentially high-powered mechanism standing idle because you haven't turned on the switch and activated the engine.

Talk about the energy crisis here on Planet Earth. We've got a crisis of Heaven's energy that makes us look like oil-rich Arabs by comparison!

Christians are literally squandering the power of God!

Through materialism.

Indifference.

Disobedience.

Now maybe—though I surely hope not—you're among those Christians content to talk about soul winning but never intending to really do anything about it. They speak out in favor of evangelism. Count on them for a few dollars in the offering plate when soul winning agencies need some support. They prefer a preacher who can really lay it on the line— especially Sunday nights when only the saints have assembled.

If you do so classify, at least you have lots of company. I can identify with your feelings, because I spent many years of my own Christian life with the same kind of motivations. You couldn't find a more faithful churchman—active in administrative affairs, in the Sunday school. I never criticized the pastor. I was strong on foreign missions.

Why, if I had died, my family could have written up an obituary that would make me look like a real saint.

But, hopefully, you are another of the sincere Christians I meet who cry out from the deepest reaches of their hearts, "I want to win souls, but I don't know how!"

How?

An important, often tantalizing, word.

Well, let's look at the "how" of winning people to Christ.

The flesh is at war against the Spirit of God. It will not cooperate with the Spirit of God. When you pray, the flesh prays only words; it is thinking about the activities of the day. When the flesh reads the Bible, it is only reading words. It doesn't want to go next door and witness, nor to the shop, the school or the office. The flesh doesn't want to be identified with Jesus Christ. That would be a reproach. It wants to be accepted by the people it works with. It wants to wear nice clothes, drive a nice car, go to nice places. It wants to be entertained and enjoy life. It just doesn't want to witness.

That's why the flesh has to become Master-controlled by the Holy Spirit. All of its faculties have to become Spirit-controlled. In other words, the flesh must no longer have any say as to what the body will do.

For example, my hand is a wonderful part of my

body. It seems that everything I do, I need my hand. When I get up in the morning, I need it to dress with. When I eat breakfast, I need it to eat with. When I go to work, I need it to drive with. When I sit at my desk, I need it to write with. But, actually, the only value the hand is to the body is when it is controlled by the head. If the hand would get puffed up and say, "I don't need the body any more," and it goes here and goes there and takes money out of my pocket without permission, it would need medical attention.

Isn't that just like the average Christian?

We don't lack for activity, we're inundated with it—and right in the heart of the ebb and flow of church affairs.

But have you taken time lately to inventory your activities? We carry a lot of items in the plastics division of our business and have had to learn that floor space and subsequent shelf space have a per-square-inch value which must not be wasted. If a product doesn't move, we *move* it—out.

Obviously, good business procedure dictates that I can't keep a product on the shelves if it isn't making money for the company.

And listen, fellow Christian, shouldn't it be far more important for me to allow no activity in my life, however noble that activity may be, if it hinders me from winning people to Christ? We are to be *not slothful in business.*[12] The Bible tells us. Our corporations net hundreds of thousands of dollars in profits every year, and we try to use that money wisely for the Lord's glory, but money and profits and all the rest are peanuts compared to the wise use of personal time and talents.

And a Christian can only wisely use his time and talents when he is Master-controlled by the Holy Spirit!

My grandfather was a magician. He and my grandmother would go in a horsedrawn spring wagon to the one room school houses in the early pioneer days of Ohio and put on entertainment for the people of the community.

When we grandchildren were young and my grandfather was old, there were long-remembered evenings when he would be in a good mood and drag out his trunk of tricks to perform for us.

We would sit eyes agape.

There was one performance I cannot forget. He had a stage where two dolls performed. He called them Punch and Judy. They were puppets. He had a place where he hid his hands with strings going to the dolls. He could throw his voice. The stage hid my Grandfather. When he would begin to manipulate his fingers and speak, we children felt as if the dolls were alive. They would do anything and say anything my grandfather wanted them to do and say, because he controlled them.

I never forgot that.

For this is what I want to be—Master-controlled by the Holy Spirit living within me. I want Him to manipulate my hands and feet. I want Him to speak through me. I want Him to win souls through me.

I want to be a soul winner who wins souls!

Don't you?

[1] Romans 8:16.
[2] Romans 8:1.
[3] Ephesians 5:18.
[4] I Corinthians 6:19.
[5] Ephesians 1:13.
[6] Ephesians 1:14.
[7] John 20:31.
[8] II Corinthians 5:17.
[9] Psalms 16:11.
[10] I Corinthians 3:15.
[11] II Timothy 4:5.
[12] Romans 12:11.

CHAPTER TWO

TIMID? FAILURE-PRONE? JOIN THE CLUB!

Fear undermines the good intentions of most Christians I meet, those who want to bring men to Christ but continually fail because they lack the necessary courage to bring Christ to men.

That's the prime function of the actual soul winning process, you know—bringing Christ to men!

Now I could take the ploy of some and, if you find yourself numbered among the failures in God's harvest field, lay you to filth for that failure. True— and you had better face up to the truth—such debilitating cancers as pride, materialism and worldliness may usurp your willingness and effectiveness in witness. But the very fact you have read this far indicates to me you more likely classify among those who do not oppose the prospect of being consistent and effective in witness. The plain facts are that you want to witness, but don't and can't quite determine what to do about it.

Well, take courage!

I can tell you right now that, if you sincerely want to be effective in your outreach to others, you can be!

When you became a Christian, you became part of the Creator's program for this earth. We are *laborers together with God.*[1] When God created Adam and Eve, His very first directive to them was *Be fruitful, and multiply, and replenish the earth.*[2]

Man obeys the fleshly aspect of that command quite effectively.

That's why we hear so much these days about population control. Unless husbands and wives limit the size of their families, the world will become so overpopulated life will be rendered impossible on this planet. I heard recently that population growth in America has now fallen to one percent and is nearing zero. I recently met one Christian couple who have decided not to have any children at all.

Well, the purpose of this book does not consist of discussing either population growth or population control.

And yet it does.

I have been in India, have seen the masses of people eking out pittance existence. An acute problem, I am told, is that religious groups distrust each other.

"You want us to limit our families," one group will say, "while you continue to increase your population. Then, a generation from now, you will overpower us with numbers."

Well, frankly, this matter of population growth keenly concerns me.

But in a bit different way.

TIMID? FAILURE-PRONE? JOIN THE CLUB!

The big Blue Marble—as an astronaut once described earth from outer space—has very definite limitations. But heaven has absolutely unlimited area and can sustain an infinite population! Who knows but what perhaps a substantial aspect of the hellishness of hell will be its overpopulation. I don't know. But I do know that the glory of heaven will consist of the multitudes of multitudes who assemble to lift their voices in praise to the lamb of God!

With each soul who makes it to Heaven, the greater will be the joy brought to the heart of our Savior—and to all of us who join Him there.

I want to help swell that population!

Now it is true that in some places across the world, many are coming to Christ. The Christian population of Indonesia increased by five million in just a few short years. Areas of Africa have a mushrooming growth of Christian population. Across the world, however, the number of people coming to Christ falls far below the annual increase in population.

Yet is it not true that every baby born into the world represents a soul winning opportunity to some Christian in the world!

Now please read carefully.

One of the dangers resident in any discussion of soul winning lies in the fact that we evangelicals have talked about it so much. Talked about it but done so little about it.

We easily grow complacent.

Russia vaulted *Sputnik* into the skies a few years ago, and the world trembled. Today outer space is a literal conglomeration of hardware, and we scarcely give it second thought.

But listen, my good friend, we had better give second thought to soul winning!

For, you see, the Christian has two specific. purposes in the world—to glorify God and to reproduce spiritually. And, while it is important to lift our hearts to God in praise, we cannot show our appreciation to Him for his grace more tangibly than in introducing that grace to others!

In this is my Father glorified, Jesus said, *"that you bear much fruit; so shall you be my diciples.*[3]

A few verses further on, Jesus said, *"You have not chosen me, but I have chosen you, and ordained you, that you should go and bring forth fruit."* [4]

What kind of fruit?

Good deeds, to be sure. The outreach of love to others. Concern for those in physical need.

But, foremost, fruit involves the winning of lost souls!

Now, then, if soul winning stands at the top of the list in our priorities as Christians, does it not appear evident that tops on Satan's list should be constant effort to keep us from winning souls?

Let me take a bold thrust further.

If you are not consistently reaching out in witness of others, serving as the very beat of God's heart to a lost world around you, the reason very likely lies in the fact of your having let Satan take control of your mind and your tongue!

Hold steady now!

I'm not accusing you of anything.

You may be an exemplary Christian in many ways. You live a moral life. You're faithful to the church·

People in the community look up to you. A few may even chide you because of your Christian convictions.

All well and good.

But I must stay with my premise. If you are not actively witnessing to those around you, daily concerned, doing something about bringing the gospel to the lost, in all likelihood Satan has control of your mind and tongue.

How can this be?

In his book on demons in the church, (*) Ken Anderson shows how deftly Satan works right in the midst of ecclesiastical activity. He doesn't possess you with demons—he can't do that, because the Holy Spirit lives within you—but he obsessess you by *the lust of the flesh, and the lust of the eyes, and the pride of life.*[5] The Apostle wrote those words to believers, not to unbelievers, for this is the way Satan attacks the Christian. And it can happen right in the heart of church activity!

And you may not even be aware of it.

How can you be aware?

Well, I just don't know of a more accurate way to assess the quality of a man's Christianity than by observing how he conducts himself in the matter of spiritual reproduction, the winning of men through personal witness.

Now please don't put down this book in disappointment and say it's no use to read further because you'll never be able to win souls.

You can win souls!

For now, let me simply suggest that you carefully

(*) SATAN'S ANGELS—A WARNING (Thomas Nelson, Inc.)

assess your mind and your motives. How high is your priority on personal witnessing? How much do you really want to bring men to the Savior? Is it the breathing, yearning, cry of your very heart?

I can tell you that, while I make no claims whatever of being any kind of a super Christian, nothing in all the world more fully occupies my mind or places more demands upon my time or effort.

So maybe you say, "But you're different, Mr. Tam. You're a successful businessman, an experienced salesman."

Don't be so sure!

I'm just an ordinary country boy from Ohio. I grew up with a fairsized inferiority complex. By nature, I lack the dynamic qualities of a successful salesman and, in my first efforts at selling, did very poorly.

A humble farm woman—whom I'll tell you more about later—led me to Christ.

It was a truly transforming experience.

God's love literally flooded my soul, making a new person out of me, changing my objectives.

And, from the very outset, I wanted to share my faith with others.

That's a characteristic trademark of the born again experience, you know—an almost instantaneous desire to share with someone else what has happened to you. *If thou shalt confess with thy mouth the Lord Jesus,* God's Word tells us, *and shalt believe in thine heart that God hath raised him from the dead, thou shalt be saved.*[6] Believing and telling go hand in hand in the Christian experience.

I'm sure you've seen it happen, possibly in your own experience. A person receives Christ. The experience is truly cataclysmic. Fearlessly, if sometimes rather tactlessly, he tells others about the experience. This is clear evidence of the Holy Spirit's working in the case of a genuine conversion.

And just as surely as this is evidence of the Holy Spirit's presence, so also is the cooling off of zeal for witnessing, evidence of Satan's intervention!

What has happened to so many others happened to me.

I made a faltering attempt at witness now and then. For the most part, though, I joined the rank and file of Christians—sure of my own faith, concerned about the needs of others, but as silent as a tombstone when it came to person-to-person witness.

I had the usual bag full of excuses.

You don't talk to people about their religious beliefs, I reasoned. That's a private matter.

If you do witness to someone, how do you explain the sorry mess we Christians are in? At odds over our different opinions of the Bible? Split up into denominations of every hue? How dare I insist my views of the Bible were correct in contrast to the somewhat differing views of another?

No, as you have perhaps told yourself more than once, it's just as well to be silent. Oh, if someone came to me and asked for spiritual guidance, I would of course give it, gladly.

Let me carefully insert another thought here.

In many evangelical churches, people are given an opportunity to give their testimony—at prayer meeting, possibly during the evening service. Far be it from me to assail such practice, for it may be very helpful, but if frightens me none-the-less.

Why?

Because I've seen people, who never open their mouths on the street or down at the office, get up and give a word of witness in church.

To whom?

To their sympathetic friends who have come to share worship or prayer and Bible study with them.

I've heard these people, then seen them sit down with a smug look of satisfaction glowing on their faces. They've witnessed. They have confessed with their mouths the Lord Jesus. And they feel they have thus discharged their responsibility.

Far better, in my opinion, would be for a pastor —or an actively witnessing layman—to take new converts out into the community, give them in-the-market place experience in declaring their faith. Then let them come back to the place of worship and share the joy of witnessing.

Missionary Dick Hillis practiced this procedure in China and later in Taiwan, with exciting results. Hubert Mitchell, the avid door-to-door evangel, brought up his children on this kind of spiritual fare.

But the average Christian?

Like me, in my early Christian walk, they are content to stand by complacently and let "George do it" when it comes to witness. Unless, of course, as I mentioned earlier, someone should happen to come and ask them how to be saved.

Well, as I became involved in selling, I soon .saw

that there is a vast difference between sitting around and waiting for business and going out and seeking it. I discovered successful selling involves being willing to fail ninety percent of the time, for it's the rare salesman—however profuse his talents—who lands more than one customer out of each ten attempts.

I became very serious about my Christian life, especially when I faced bankruptcy and—in desparation—promised God I'd turn everything over to Him. God came to my rescue. The business thrived. I gave profusely to Christian causes.

But there was an emptiness in the pit of my soul.

Because, you see, a Christian can only find true fulfillment by sharing his faith with others. And—I cannot over-emphasize it—the human emotions were so designed by our Creator so that our greatest joy comes only when we succeed in leading another human being to a personal knowledge of Jesus Christ.

In the ensuing chapters, I'd like to share with you the way God has led me into His exciting, rewarding harvest field.

I do it with the prayer that you, too, may begin soon to experience the matchless joy of bringing lost men to a saving relationship with Jesus Christ!

[1] I Corinthians 3:9.
[2] Genesis 1:28.
[3] John 15:8.
[4] John 15:16.
[5] John 2:16.
[6] Romans 10:9.

CHAPTER THREE

RUNNING SCARED, BUT RUNNING

Timidity is the norm for the beginning soul winner, often the continuing problem of veterans in the harvest. So if you find yourself running short on courage at the thought of witnessing, much less the act, don't throw in the sponge.

Actually, lack of courage becomes a source of strength. Seems like a paradox? It isn't. For when you sense the lack of your own resources, that's when you turn to a source of supply beyond yourself. And this is exactly what you must learn to do in witnessing.

People who have a clever wit, who have a natural knack for chatter, who think quickly on their feet, are no more sure of success in soul winning than the shy person. Both must permit the Holy Spirit to flow through them. And the shy person, by virtue of so keenly realizing his lack, turns to the Lord for strength more quickly than the strongly secure person.

Remember, the Holy Spirit within you—not you
—performs the function of soul winning!

Then, too, shyness is a human trait, therefore a
weakness of the flesh. And you'll remember back in
Chapter One that we said the flesh must be Master-
controlled by the Holy Spirit.

So, first off, if you're shy, if you're downright
frightened, tell God. Admit to the flesh-impetus of
this weakness.

And determine all the more to be Master-controlled!

Your prayer could go something like this:

> Lord, I'm just plain scared to talk to people
> about You. Yet I want to. With all my heart
> I want to. I believe the Holy Spirit gave me
> the desire to witness, and I'm thankful for
> that desire. Now, Lord, by faith I turn my
> body—my mind, my lips—over to the Holy
> Spirit. I will depend upon Him to lead me, to
> give me courage greater than my shyness, to—
> most important of all—cause the Lord Jesus
> Christ to be glorified through everything in
> my life.

You may want to phrase the prayer in your own
words. That's much better. The important thing is
to do it, to really turn yourself over to the control of
the Holy Spirit.

Do it daily.

Do it throughout the day, whenever you sense the
need of strength and guidance.

Now let me share something I've observed through
the years. Something of which you may also be

aware. Such a trait as shyness may hide fine talent deep within some people.

Perhaps in music, in some other form of art, or in the business and technical world, they could have excelled if somehow they had been helped onto the right track.

The talent was there but it was latent talent.

The same holds true in soul winning. However timid you may be, so timid that you may have never tried to win someone to Christ, the fact remains that you could have the talent to be one of God's most effective witnesses!

Programs like the Dale Carnige course and the Toastmaster's Club have brought multitudes of people out of their timid shells. How much more likely then that the Holy Spirit can deliver a child of God from the crippling terrors of fear and give him courage and strength far beyond his natural capactiy.

But you must let the Holy Spirit do it, not try to attain in your own strength.

To do this you need complete honesty.

As I indicated in the initial chapter, your problem could be that of spiritual disobedience. If so, don't waste another moment. Cry out to God for forgiveness. Confess your sins, identifying them by name. The Bible speaks to Christians when it says, *If we confess our sins, He is faithful and just to forgive us our sins, and to cleanse us from all unrighteousness.*[1]

But the fact you have read this far into the book more likely indicates a different situation. You do seek to live above sin in this sinful world. You do want God to be glorified in every event of your life.

You are deeply concerned about your failure in witnessing and just as deeply determined to do something about it.

Let me share what happened to me.

As a young man, I got into the silver reclamation business. I had secured the rights from an inventor by the name of Aukerman to manufacture a device which collected residue silver from photo processing tanks. During the first years the business went very poorly. At the verge of bankruptcy, God led me into the enriching experience of literally, legally, making Him my equal partner. Subsequently, my wife and I turned all of the stock of our company over to the Lord.

Immediately, we checked our losses, became solvent, and then the business began to grow. It was nothing short of miraculous.

I served as Sunday school superintendent in our church, had great plans for encouraging growth. During the first year, however, our average enrollment dropped rather than increased.

It stung my pride.

Wasn't I a success in business, with people talking about how I had set an example of good stewardship by making God my co-partner? Didn't I utilize sales techniques which caused the business to prosper? If I could successfully build a business, why couldn't I successfully build a Sunday school?

Lima, Ohio, where we live, is only a couple of hours drive from the famous Bible conference grounds in Winona Lake, Indiana. One summer, as my wife and I attended the conference, I browsed in the book store. My eye fell upon the title of a book.

How To Put Your Sunday School Across.

Exactly what I needed!

As I picked up the book, however, and turned to make my way to the sales counter, another book caught my eye. Strangely, I noticed the name of the author more than the title of the book.

Charles Finney.

I bought both books.

I read the book on Sunday schools, found many helpful ideas, but it was Finney's book that literally ignited my heart. Through one chapter, titled "Hinderance to Revival," I took a new look at myself. Oh, I was a separated Christian, a Bible student, active in my church—and so very proud of the fact!

Many lives have been transformed at Winona Lake through the years, often at the close of an evangelistic rally in the Billy Sunday Tabernacle. But I walked out along the lake shore, found a place where I could be completely by myself.

That spot became hallowed ground.

I invited the Holy Spirit to search my heart, to place the finger of conviction upon anything which might hinder my effectiveness as a Sunday school worker.

What happened?

Attendance grew until, within the next twelve months, we doubled our Sunday school enrollment. And the growth continued.

Subsequently, I attended a Sunday school conference in Chicago. The sessions invigorated me, every speaker pulsating with new ideas I could incorporate into our program back in Lima.

Nights, however, I spent in my hotel room.

With my Bible.

For the first time, I began to face squarely what the Bible said about personal witness.

Ye shall receive power, after the Holy Spirit has come upon you; and ye shall be witnesses unto me.[2]

He that gathereth in summer is a wise son, but he that sleepest in harvest is a son that causeth shame.[3]

The fruit of the righteous is a tree of life; and he that winneth souls is wise.[4]

I felt strangely troubled.

And it bothered me.

Why should verses like these bring conviction to my heart? Look how our Sunday school had grown, I reasoned. By virtue of having made God my business partner, my wife and I were channeling substantial sums of money into missionary work. I maybe didn't reach people for Christ on a man-to-man basis but, on the other hand, you could hardly say I was one of those asleep during harvest.

Or could you?

"I want *you* to be a soul winner, Stanley," the Lord seemed to say. "I've helped you overcome shyness, and given you the talents for selling merchandise. Now I want you to use this talent to persuade men of their need for salvation."

Strange, isn't it, how upended we can become sometimes, when the Holy Spirit begins to deal with us?

You may be experiencing similar emotion just now.

If so, be encouraged!

The Holy Spirit rarely deals with those who permit the cares of this world, the lusts of this life, to take preeminence in their thoughts. It is only as we recognize our need, as we reach out to God in confession and penitence, that the Holy Spirit is most likely to disturb our complacency.

As I wrestled with conviction in that hotel room, I didn't want to resist the voice of the Holy Spirit. With all my heart, I wanted to be whatever God wanted me to be. My problem was fear. For I am by nature a shy introvert. Approaching people on a person-to-person basis just doesn't come natural to me.

I spent several days at that convention. But I found myself less and less able to concentrate on Sunday school matters. This strong conviction lingered in my heart, the sense of awareness that God wanted me to reach out to lost men on a personal basis.

One night I went for a long walk. There were quite a number of people on the streets in the downtown area. I wanted to stop each one of them, to ask him if he knew Christ as his personal savior, if he wanted to know Him.

How wonderful if I could speak to just one of them.

But I didn't speak to anybody. The very thought of bearing personal witness to a stranger struck terror deep into my heart.

Fear, yes, but even stronger than fear came the growing desire—a desire which was like anguish—to somehow break free from my cowardice and dare to give my witness.

If there had been a Salvation Army group on one of those street corners, with a few dozen people listening to their music and witness, I could have joined the group. I could have given a testimony. Person-to-person, however, would have been quite something else.

In my long walk that evening, I came to the theater district—brilliant marquees featuring the latest Hollywood releases, the names of famous stars.

An idea re-awakened in my mind.

I had previously given thought to securing a motion picture projector and using Christian films in house-to-house evangelism. In the past, when this idea came, fear squelched it.

But that night, back in my hotel room, I fortified my faith through the Gideon Bible, then dropped to my knees by the bed.

"You have not chosen me," Jesus told his disciples and us, *"but I have chosen you, and ordained you, that you should go and bring forth fruit, and that your fruit should remain; that whatsoever you shall ask of your Father in my name, He may give it to you."* [5]

"Lord," I prayed, as sincerely and expectantly as I had ever prayed in my whole life, "you say you chose me and ordained me to bear fruit. You also invite me to ask for what I need, so I can effectively bear fruit. Well, Lord, I'm a coward. I need courage. Please help me!"

God answered that prayer.

Courage came to my heart, only a breath at first, but the courage grew, giving birth to vision and determination.

My friends back in Lima discouraged the idea of motion picture evangelism, when I told them about it.

"We need you giving all your spare time to develop the Sunday school," they said.

"Are you sure people will let you come into their homes just to show movies?" others asked. "Wouldn't it be better to invite them to attend Sunday school and church?"

I listened to the arguments. I want always to be open to the counsel of others. I never want to be bull headed. But I was absolutely sure God had spoken to me.

So I secured a projector and a couple of films. But then I realized I had no invitations to show the film. I didn't know of one home where I might go. I surely didn't have the courage to simply walk up to a house, projector in hand, and ring the doorbell.

I shared my vision and dilemma with our wonderful pastor. He had encouraged me when others threw cold water on my idea.

"What about all the contacts you've made through the Sunday school?" he asked. "Aren't there a lot of parents who willingly send their children to Sunday school but never darken the door of our church themselves?"

It was just the impetus I needed!

In one evening, I drew up a sizeable list. Then, selecting a family likely to be cooperative, I made the first telephone call.

My knees trembled and, when someone answered, my breath shortened. But I managed to stammer. "Uh, this is Stanley Tam here in Lima. Your children, Bobby and Denise, attend our Sunday school. I'm superintendent. I've got a couple of short films to show in your home. Would you let me come some evening?"

Whew!

One of the hardest things I ever did!

But, to my sheer delight, they welcomed the idea.

I didn't become an expert overnight. Not by any means. A successful soul winner needs to be able to speak fluently and unoffensively to people. I had neither the desire nor the ability to bluntly ask people to receive Christ on those first encounters.

Yet I knew I had to bring people to a place of personal decision.

I did notice one encouraging trend. When I took the films into a home, people were invariably on guard. Some would go to considerable pains to tell me how good they were, how they had really never done anything displeasing to God. But then, as I showed a film, as we chatted afterward, the defense mechanism would break down.

I learned that most people want to talk to someone about their spiritual lives. When they learned that I wasn't some kind of religious nut, that I was a successful businessman in town with a deep assurance of God's presence in my own life which I wanted to share with others, they opened up in response.

I went to several homes, showed the films again and again, invited the people to attend our church.

Many did.

But I wanted them to take that further step, to winsomely and effectively invite the Lord Jesus Christ into their very lives.

Oh, I had read the words of the Apostle Paul where he said, *"I have planted, Apollos watered, but*

*God gave the increase. So, then, neither is he that
planted anything, neither he that watereth, but God
that giveth the increase."* 6

Sometimes it takes several encounters with personal witness from several different sources before a
man or a woman will break down spiritual resistence
and turn to the Lord. But I wanted, at least once in
a while, to be the one who experienced this actual
harvest!

Extremely shy at first, I couldn't bring myself to
ask for that all-important decision. But, with each
visit, I gained confidence. Then, too, the more homes
I visited, the more additional contacts I made. At
first, I set aside two nights a week. Soon, however, it
became necessary to add another night.

At the beginning of my visits, I depended entirely
upon the message of the films to present the gospel.
Little by little, growing bolder, I began presenting
the way of salvation myself.

It was so thrilling to open my Bible and say, "You
know, first of all, the Bible teaches us we are all
sinners. Here in Romans 3:23, it says, *all have sinned
and come short of the glory of God.* That means
everyone of us in this room.

"That's why the Lord Jesus came into the world.
The heart of the Gospel is found over here in the
fifteenth chapter of first Corinthians, where the
Apostle Paul writes: *Moreover, brethren, I declare
unto you the gospel . . . that Christ died for our sins
according to the scriptures; and that he was buried,
and that he rose again the third day according to the
scriptures.*

"Now, of course, we've got to realize that we can't

do anything to save ourselves. *Not by works of right-eousness which we have done,* it says here in Titus 3:5, *but according to his mercy he saved us.*

"So how can we be saved? God tells us right here in Romans 10:13, *whosoever shall call upon the name of the Lord shall be saved.* And over here in the first chapter of John, the twelfth verse, *as many as received him* . . . that's the Lord Jesus the Bible is talking about . . . *to them gave he power to become the sons of God, even to them that believe on his name.*"

Then, finally, came that first, wonderful experience!

I visited a home where the mother was a believer, the husband not. As I showed one of the films, I kept glancing at the father, saw how deeply impressed he was. I cried out to God in desperate silence—for the man, that he would open his heart to Christ, but also for myself, that I would have the courage to speak boldly with him about his spiritual need.

I had no more than turned on the lights at the conclusion of the film when the man said, "You know, I attended Sunday school regularly when I was a kid. I memorized Bible verses. I recognized some of them in that film you just showed us. But it's a funny thing. In all those years of attending Sunday school, even church sometimes, nobody ever asked me if I wanted to be a Christian. If anybody had, I just might've become one."

Summoning every ounce of courage in my heart, I said, "You could invite Christ into your heart to-night, just as you saw the man do in the film."

"Do it, Frank," his wife whispered tenderly.

And Frank did!

For the very first time in my life, I had the joy of leading a man to Christ!

I can hardly remember the minor details of that night. I don't think I broke any speed limits driving home. But, I tell you, that car seemed to float above the street on wings.

My wife shared my ecstacy, as I told her what had happened.

"I led a man to Christ, Honey!" I exclaimed. "Can you believe that I sat right there beside him and showed him in the Bible how to ask the Lord into his life! And he did it!"

It was indescribable, the joy in my heart. In spite of my timidity, my faltering tongue, God had used me to bring about the salvation of a lost soul for whom the Lord Jesus Christ hung on the cross.

Sure, I was timid, still running scared, but I was running.

And I didn't intend to stop!

[1] I John 1:9.
[2] Acts 1:8.
[3] Proverbs 10:5.
[4] Proverbs 11:30.
[5] John 15:16.
[6] I Corinthians 3:6, 7.

CHAPTER FOUR

NOTHING SUCCEEDS LIKE SUCCESS

Winning that first man to Christ was like taking the first step on a glorious ladder upward.

No longer could I say, "I can't lead a soul to Christ."

Because I had led one!

Until that triumphant experience, I was all but overcome by timidity whenever I took my projector to a house and rang the doorbell.

But I shall always remember the next appointment, after that milestone experience. I returned from work and came bounding into the house. Juanita, my lovely wife, could see the difference success had made. I have no idea what we had for dinner that night, though my wife is an excellent cook, because I wanted to get eating out of the way and go calling.

There was a bounce in my step, as I took the projector from the car and walked up to the home of one of our Sunday school children.

I didn't win any of that family to Christ that night.

The Holy Spirit used me in seed sowing and nurturing. But my courage sustained. And, one evening shortly afterward, another precious soul came to my Savior.

Then another.

And another.

I was still Stanley Tam, the shy one. But confidence in the guidance and the wisdom of the Holy Spirit, bolstered by living proof that God honors the spreading of His Word, gave me more and more courage.

The best way I can describe the joy of leading someone to Christ is to call it a kind of divine ecstasy. There's nothing in life to compare it to, for it is an emotion all its own.

I don't know what moves you. Perhaps a great musical rendition. Or standing in an art gallery and looking at a Rembrandt original or something from the brush of Cezanne or Van Goh. Well, imagine the emotion of the artists themselves when they created something of beauty.

But nothing—absolutely nothing—quite compares with the thrill of helping a sinner fix his eyes on the Lord Jesus Christ, so he can be lifted out of the miry pit of sin and placed on the solid rock!

As we shall consider more fully later, you come into unique rapport with the Creator when you win a soul. *If any man be in Christ,* the Bible tells us, *he is a new creation; old things are passed away; behold, all things are become new.*[1] You help bring into being *a new creation* when you lead a man to Christ!

But though there is great joy in soul winning, it is not a trivial experience. It's not like yelling your lungs out at a football game, because your team won. Not like floating on air all the way home from the office because you got a big raise.

Soul winning involves work.

It involves you, deeply.

It also requires disciplined obedience.

Do you wonder why we have so much unhappiness in the world, so many confused people, so many neurotics? The major thrust of our problem lies in the breakdown of authority.

People don't want to obey the law. Children don't want to obey their parents or their teachers at school. We want to do our own thing, to have our own way, be our own boss.

But obedience provides us with one of the most effective and lasting sources of emotional security in life.

Occasionally salesmen come into my office and throw a big line. Judge them by what they say, by the vanity they express on the outside, and you would call them highly secure individuals. When I talk to such men, however, I try to do a bit of digging. Often it doesn't take much time to get down beneath the veneer to the real man.

The one who blows his trumpet the loudest is often the one who has the least air in his lungs.

I believe God designed us this way.

Purposely.

God doesn't want us to feel security in ourselves.

He wants us to depend on Him.

45

And that's why He made us so that, in ourselves, we can never quite put it all together. Nor can we attain true fulfillment in life simply by occasionally genuflecting to the Almighty for an hour on Sunday morning.

Pascal, the famous French philosopher, said, "Every man is born with a God-shaped vacuum inside."

And we can't fill that vacuum by trying to relate to God on our terms. No, if we are to experience genuine spiritual life, we must meet God on His terms!

When the ecclesiastical leaders of the first century put the pressure on the early apostles, commanding them not to preach and teach in the name of Jesus, Peter and his associates responded in a unified voice, *"We ought to obey God rather than man."* [2]

Obedience!

That's the key!

You want to be at peace with God? You want to experience real serenity in your life? You want good relationships with others?

It all begins with your relationship to God!

And the key to a right relationship to God lies dead center down the highway of obedience!

Do you see how it fits together?

God did not put you in this world to please yourself. You are no genetic accident. God has a plan for your life and He wants you to discover *what is that good, and acceptable, and perfect, will of God.* [3]

And the function of spiritual reproduction lies basic to God's prime purpose in placing you in this world. He doesn't ask you to reproduce by your own initiative. You don't go out blindly ringing doorbells, as a salesman might do.

The Holy Spirit indwells you, remember?

And the Holy Spirit alone can bring men to Christ, not you. You simply provide the instrument through which the Holy Spirit works.

You do this by obedience, which is the key to being Master-controlled by the Holy Spirit.

But what is obedience?

I've met Christians who believe obedience to God consists of much prayer. Hear me out completely, before you put down this book, but I'm afraid sometimes people use prayer as a cop-out to real obedience. For, as I study my Bible, I find the word obedience strategically linked to another word.

Initiative.

Harness those two forces in your life . . . obedience and initiative . . . and, even if you were born the world's greatest coward, you can be a success for God!

I do believe in prayer.

For years, I've cultivated the habit of rising a half hour ahead of the family every morning for Bible study and prayer.

But when I pray, I make it very clear to God that I want to be His instrument for that day. Prayer then does not serve as a shelter from the world but a launching platform out into the world. During that time of prayer, searching the Scriptures, the Holy Spirit renews my confidence, bolsters my courage, fortifies me with the promises of the Bible.

God is on my side. The Bible is my authority. The Holy Spirit is my strength, my wisdom.

So how can I help but succeed?

But obedience lies bedrock to success as a Christian. That's why, from the first prayer of the day, I invite the Holy Spirit's guidance. I look for those Bible verses which give me direction. Prayer is a time to praise God, I know. And the Bible instills worship. But, foremost in my experience, Bible study and prayer must be linked to my willingness to obey the Holy Spirit's promptings in my life.

How wonderful it is to search out the motivational truths of the Word of God.

Delight thyself also in the Lord, the Bible invites us, *and he shall give thee the desires of thine heart. Commit thy way unto the Lord; trust also in Him, and he shall bring it to pass.*[4]

The desires of thine heart.

What does that mean?

Everything your heart desires?

Hardly.

Literally, Bible scholars tell us, the implication of the verse is that, as we delight ourselves in the Lord, He gives us the desires that should be in our hearts. These desires, given to us by the Holy Spirit, become our motivation.

So, as I talk to my Lord each morning, I ask Him anew for the desire to see men brought to Christ. The Holy Spirit answers that prayer, fanning the flame of spiritual desire in my heart. Thus it becomes impossible for me to leave the house, see people go to and fro in our town, and have no thought of their spiritual need. I couldn't think of getting on an airplane, as I do just about every weekend of my life, sit down beside someone and not be conscious of the fact that he may have deep spiritual needs to which I can relate.

The Holy Spirit, the one who brings men to Christ through us, gives me this desire.

He will do the same for you!

Desire then begets initiative. When I'm hungry, I desire food, and so I take the initiative to get food, to satiate the hunger. When I want fellowship, I desire the presence of other Christians, and so I take the initiative to put myself with other Christians.

God tells us in His word that *we are His workmanship, created in Christ Jesus unto good works, which God hath before ordained we should walk in them.*[5]

Desire begets initiative, then, and initiative is taken as a direct result of obedience. They inter relate like the fabric in a fine cloth.

How do you perform work without initiative?

"Work doesn't bother me," a jokester once said. "I can lie right down beside of it and fall fast asleep."

It's the same with the carnal Christian. He can "sleep" his way through a complacent, fruitless life, unless he permits the Holy Spirit to cleanse His life of fleshly indifference and set him aflame with the desire to be one of God's effective workmen.

But once you begin to serve God, in obedience, with initiative, this obedience and initiative stimulate momentum.

I'm amazed as I look at the growth of our business. From those struggling early years, beginning in the humblest of surroundings, we now have a multimillion-dollar-a-year enterprise. States Smelting, our initial silver reclaiming business, gave birth to US Plastics. Then, more recently, we began a mail order business, and it's doing exceedingly well.

You see, after Juanita and I turned everything over to the Lord, the silver business began to succeed. That created momentum for the plastics business. And, as momentum grew, we saw the opportunity for the direct mail business.

Success generates success.

You'll find it the same in soul winning.

Once you get that taste of winning one soul, you'll want to win another. Your confidence will increase. Sheer momentum will carry you on from outreach to outreach.

Jesus said, *"Follow me, and I will make you fishers of men."* [6] Did you ever hear of a fisherman who rowed out into the middle of a lake, cast, promptly caught a big one and immediately rowed back to shore and called it a day?

Of course not!

If there's one big fish out there, there must be another.

And more.

Soul winning, of course, isn't some kind of sport. It's no game. It's mighty serious business.

But it's no hyper-pious, long-faced enterprise. You point out the fact of sin, of course, but your prime purpose is to introduce people to the Lord Jesus Christ. He said, *I am come that they might have life, and that they might have it more abundantly.*[7]

You'll meet people with deep guilt complexes.

You'll help them discover that, *as far as the east is from the west, so far hath he removed our transgressions from us.*[8]

You'll see people released from the chains of habit, because *if the Son, therefore, shall make you free, ye shall be free indeed.*[9]

You'll see marriages, on the brink of divorce, magnificently restored *for love shall cover a multitude of sins.*[10]

You'll see families, riven by discord, brought into harmony by becoming *exceedingly abundant with faith and love which is in Christ Jesus.*[11]

Nothing long-faced about those kind of experiences!

And the more you walk with the Lord, the more experience you have in relating your faith to others, the more adept you will be in witness. Just because the Holy Spirit indwells us doesn't mean we become automatic in effective witness.

We are human.

Grow in grace, and in the knowledge of our Lord and Savior Jesus Christ,[12] the Apostle Peter wrote. In his earlier epistle, He wrote, *as newborn babes, desire the pure milk of the word, that you may grow by it.*[13]

Walking with the Lord, witnessing to those who do not know him, involves a thrilling process of growth.

We also learn from each other. Someone just beginning to venture forth in the harvest field, sowing the good seed of God's word and gathering in those who want to receive the Savior into their lives, can learn from others more experienced in spiritual service.

I've been involved in personal evangelism since 1945. I've made my share of mistakes. I'm learning new things all the time.

Perhaps, through sharing some of the things I've learned, I can be of help to you.

Just fasten securely in your mind this one truth. No matter how shy you are, how inexperienced, how impossible it may seem for you to reach out and touch the other in effective Christian witness, you can do it.

If I could, you can.

And when you do, victory will lead to victory, joy to joy, because—especially when you do business with God, nothing succeeds like success!

[1] II Corinthians 5:17.
[2] Acts 5:29.
[3] Romans 12:2.
[4] Psalm 37:4-5.
[5] Ephesians 2:10.
[6] Matthew 1:19.
[7] John 10:10.
[8] Psalms 103:12.
[9] Psalms 8:36.
[10] 1 Peter 4:8.
[11] I Timothy 1:14.
[12] II Peter 3:18.
[13] I Peter 2:2.

CHAPTER FIVE

SIX POINTS FOR SUCCESSFUL WITNESSING

Maybe you've read some of the many books on soul winning. I've read a few. And a lot of these books are good. Some excellent. But you can read them all —memorize them—and never become a soul winner.

Not without a plan.

That word "plan," if you're a mainline evangelical, probably has you looking for a red flag to wave or a hold button to push.

I don't blame you.

You've been to Bible conferences, listened to revival speakers, heard scores of Sunday sermons—all of which urged you to throw off your lethargy and become an active soul winner. To help you accomplish your goal, the speakers often suggested a plan.

Perhaps rarely the same plan.

But before you close this book and turn on the TV set, let me give you something to think about. Every one of those plans put forth may have been a good plan. Many of them may have worked for you.

Because, you see, there's no one locked in method for approaching a lost soul, winning his confidence, giving him the gospel and bringing him to Christ.

The reason I say you must have a plan is because few if any worthy enterprises in this life ever succeed without one.

I once heard of a farmer who attended evangelistic services in a country schoolhouse. The impact of the gospel cut him to the quick. But, possessed of a hard-nosed disposition by nature, he refused to respond to the evangelist's altar call.

He couldn't shake off the Holy Spirit's deep conviction on his heart, however. One afternoon out plowing, the weight of that conviction became so intense he stopped his team of horses alongside a lonely fence row, dropped to his knees and opened his heart to Christ.

He became an ardent witness, going about the community in his spare time to tell others what had happened to him.

Whenever he found someone who wanted to be converted, he took him out to the same fence row where he had had his experience. The "plan" worked for him and so he insisted on it for everyone else!

Now there may have been nothing at all wrong with this farmer's plan. Or, as I say, the plans of the many speakers you've heard.

The important thing is for you to have a plan personalized for you by the Holy Spirit!

Permit me to insert a paragraph here and say that I've only decided to write a book, in response to hundreds of requests for such a book, simply because it isn't possible to share with everyone personally as I would like. So, if you can, as you read this book please try to think of the two of us sitting face-to-face in shared conversation. Because that's the way I wish it could be. This book is only second best.

With very few exceptions, every Friday night or Saturday morning finds me boarding a plane and heading out somewhere across North America—and occasionally across the world—to share my concern for effective personal evangelism. I'm grateful to God for the many churches, the many pastors and lay leaders, who invite me to their communities and give me the opportunity of sharing my experiences and convictions.

My procedure on such occasions is to present a plan involving six rules for effective soul winning.

Now, as I indicated a few paragraphs back, please don't think that I have any intention of imposing these rules on you. Far better for you to search out the scriptures for yourself, to seek the Holy Spirit's guidance, and then, in obedience with initiative, witness as you are led to do.

But perhaps you can glean something from my experiences.

Before I give you these rules, however, I want to share a basic premise.

You must keep a tender spirit toward the spiritual needs of every human being in the world, and a particular concern that you may be sensitive to the needs of those who cross your path. Complacency is a more common malady for the average Christian than the common cold. Slack up on your Bible study, become casual in your prayer life, and you will surely lose your zeal for soul winning.

I often sense carelessness and lack of concern for the lost in my own life.

All too often.

Whenever this happens, I apply a time-tested remedy. I get out my Bible and read everything I can find in it which speaks of hell and the eternal condemnation of those who are not born again. This always renews my burden for those who are lost.

A consuming burden for souls and a clean life are the two imperatives for consistent, effective soul winning.

Now for the six rules.

1. Lean on a person, the Holy Spirit within you, to do the job.
2. Remember that the greatest victories are always preceded by prayer.
3. Use "test" questions to open up a conversation.
4. Keep alert.
5. Look at inconveniences as potential opportunities.
6. Remember that soul winning takes time.

God is a God of order. He does everything according to a plan. Look up at the stars on the next clear night—as their varying brightness greets us from hundreds to multiplied thousands of light years out into space. Yet every detail of that magnificent panorama, every cubic inch, was pre-planned by our redeeming Creator.

His word counsels us to be *not slothful in business*.[1]

Well, the greatest business in all the world is winning men to Christ. It involes the most valuable merchandise, promising the greatest service to mankind, and pays higher dividends than anything else you can possibly do.

So lets look at the six rules.

> First: *Lean on a person, the Holy Spirit within you, to do the job.*

Too many Christians settle for a do-it-yourself brand of faith. Don't fall into that error. You in yourself can only generate human loyalty, human concern, human courage.

Satan himself opposes you, when you set out to share your faith with others. He wants you to be phony. He doesn't want you to succeed.

So how can you possibly make it with your own natural resources?

No, you must have courage and wisdom beyond your natural propensity.

More distinctly than any other earthly endeavor, witnessing is God's work. Just as you could never create a living tree, so you cannot bring redemption to a living soul.

You must let the Holy Spirit do this through you! How?

From the moment you arise in the morning until you go to sleep at night, depend upon the Holy Spirit's guidance. You don't need to be some wild-eyed mystic to do this. Depending upon the Holy

Spirit, who indwells every Christian, should be as natural to our spiritual lives as breathing is to our physical lives.

You put your thoughts, by faith, into the Holy Spirit's control. Thus your sensitivity, your sense of alertness, your tactfulness—everything required for effective witnessing comes under the control of a power and a mind far beyond your own.

I was invited to go to Findlay, Ohio, thirty miles north of where I live, to speak in a large liberal church. I was in prayer that God would give me a soul out of this meeting.

When the night came, it was a bad night—raining, freezing, blowing—and I hesitated to make the trip thinking that so few would come to the meeting. However, I went and not many people did come, perhaps about thirty.

I gave my testimony, looking to God for a soul in answer to my prayers, but no opportunity developed. I hung around and was about the last to leave. As I went out the door, the janitor locked it behind me. It was about ten o'clock and, as I made my way to my automobile in the parking lot, I met a lady.

"I want to thank you for coming on such a bad night to speak to us," she said. Then she added, "I'm not happy."

"What do you mean, you're not happy?" I asked.

"You asked a question tonight that I can't say yes to."

"What question was that?"

"You asked us, if we died tonight, would we go to heaven, and the answer to that question for me is no."

Well, what do you do with a lady in a parking lot at ten o'clock at night, when the wind is blowing, it's dark and the janitor has locked the church door? Do you say, "Well, lady, I hope you make it to heaven," and drive away?

You can't do that.

Should you invite her over into your automobile and say we'll talk some more about this? I'm a married man, she's a married woman, and I'm no prude but I do stick to good ethics.

"Lord," I prayed, "what should I do with this lady?"

Then the answer came.

"Is your husband with you tonight?"

"Oh, yes, he's over in the car waiting for me."

"Would he mind if you would invite me over to your house and we could talk further?"

"Oh, no, Mr. Tam, he's as interested and mixed up as I am."

"Would you invite me over?"

"It would be asking too much on such a bad night and you have a long way to go."

"You just ask me."

I followed them home. That night I shared my experience with them and then took the Word of God and showed them the plan of Salvation.

At midnight they knelt by their davenport inviting Christ to come into their hearts and lives.

I have been in that home many times since then and God has given them a vital testimony.

The Holy Spirit had definitely guided me!

Let's look at the next rule.

Second: *Remember that the greatest victories are always preceded by prayer.*

I personally like to kneel when I pray.

But I also believe in prayer on the run.

Pray without ceasing,[2]   the Bible tells us. That verse means precisely what it says. Live in a constant attitude of prayer.

But you also need times of concerted prayer.

Why not put down this book right now for a few moments? Quietly admit to God your faults, your weaknesses, any sin you know should be taken from your life. Tell Him how much you want to be a fruitful Christian through obedience to the Holy Spirit.

Spend some moments recognizing the power of the Holy Spirit. He is the power exercised in creation.[3] Through Him God communicated His message to us in the inspired scriptures.[4] And the miracle of the incarnation, by which God became man and wrought our redemption, was the distinct work of the Holy Spirit.[5]

Recognize that, even as God did his work through the Holy Spirit in creation, in giving us our Bible, in the virgin birth, in many multiplied other ways, so His divine plan is for you to permit the Holy Spirit to flow creatively out of your life in witnessing to others.

In simple prayer, tell God you want this to happen in your life. Invite the Holy Spirit to guide you, to be the master of your conscience, to own your energy, your initiative.

Then, too, you will want specific times of prayer,

not only in a more general way. Renew your commitment daily. But be much in prayer over specific concerns, definite people whom the Holy Spirit places on your heart.

Let me suggest an example of how this might happen.

Your neighbor for whom you have a deep concern. First and foremost, pray. Pray for your neighbor of course. But, most important, pray for yourself!

Actually, the Bible says very little about praying for those who are lost. But it says a lot about praying for those who reach out in witness to the lost!

So, as you pray for yourself, tell the Holy Spirit you want to be obedient, to be available as His instrument in reaching your neighbors. Then, when you have encounters with your neighbors, quietly invite the Holy Spirit to tell you what you should say, how to see the opportunities for witness when they are presented.

It is especially important for you to tell God you will obey the promptings of the Holy Spirit.

And, most important of all when you pray, ask God to place a deep burden upon your heart for those who are lost.

He that goeth forth and weepeth, our Bible tells us, *bearing precious seed, shall doubtless come again with rejoicing, bringing his sheaves with him.*[6] I believe the word "weepeth" here speaks of a real burden for prayer. As I know you realize, soul winning is no casual matter.

The above verse especially applies to those whom you may have contacted, given your witness, but who continue to reject the Lord. You have sown the seed but have seen no harvest.

My home town of Lima, Ohio, is in the heart of a rich agricultural community. We see the farmers plant their crops and then watch over those crops until they're safe in the barn. If it's a dry year, the farmer listens intently to weather forecasts, goes out in the morning and surveys the sky for any hint of rain. Dare the soul winner have any less concern for his planting and harvest?

I remember Bill, an ex-Army captain, who one day appeared at our Sunday school with his children. Thinking his coming indicated spiritual interest, I called at his home.

Bill's wife met me at the door.

"I've come hoping to give your husband some spiritual encouragement," I said.

"My husband?" She laughed as though I had just given her the punch line of a joke. "If he's spiritual, I'm Marilyn Monroe!"

"But he brought your children with him to Sunday school yesterday."

"Sure," she said, quieting a bit. "Look, he hates Sunday school, doesn't have an ounce of interest in the church."

"Then why . . ."

"He wanted to buy some fishing tackle out of the budget. I told him if he'd take the kids to Sunday school for three months he could have the money."

I asked if I might see her husband and she invited me into the house. I found him to be exactly as she pictured him.

Yet carefully, silently praying for guidance, I

talked with Bill. I reminded him of his responsibility to be a good example to his children. I showed him the plan of salvation.

We talked for quite some time. There were moments when he seemed almost interested.

Then he abruptly looked at his watch and said, "It's time for the ten o'clock news. I don't want to talk religion any more."

So I left.

But what a burden I had for Bill's soul! I can't say I wept actual tears but my heart ached for that man. I spent hours in prayer for him. At work, even in the busiest times of the day, the Holy Spirit brought him to my mind, and I had to clear my thoughts and take a few moments to do nothing but pray.

He continued to bring the children to Sunday school. (I guess he really wanted that fishing tackle.) But he kept his distance from me.

One day the burden became so heavy I again called at the home.

He came to the door himself, having seen me drive up, and I'll always remember the look on his face.

He was a new man!

Alone there in the house, he had opened his heart to the Savior just two days before!

The day came when this man, who attended Sunday school on a strange arrangement with his wife, became our Sunday school superintendent.

How very important it is for us to make our witness a matter of much prayer!

Soul winning isn't something you plunge into.

You become God's surgeon when you witness. You don't plunge the dagger into a prospect, you deftly wield the knife.

Which leads me to an important matter.

Now it can certainly be true in your case that the Lord would lead you to situations where you might go to a person and immediately begin sharing your faith. If you do, however, be absolutely sure of the Holy Spirit's guidance. You must not—repeat: *must not*—try to witness in the energy of your own flesh.

More likely you will find your witness opportunities by keeping alert for natural openings through which you can reach out and touch the lives of others.

Which lead us to the next rule.

Third: *Use "test" questions to open up a conversation.*

You can exercise conversational control when you talk to people. But one must be infinitely careful in doing so. *Let your speech be always with grace, seasoned with salt,*[7] the Bible says. Your speech is the show window of your personality. To be an effective soul winner, you must exercise good speech habits.

As some people usually insist on doing all the talking, whatever you do, avoid being such a person. As a matter of fact, I have found that soul winning involves knowing how to listen constructively.

But you can't listen all the time.

You must come to the point where you are in control of the conversation.

So let me give you a simple illustration of how conversational control works.

Let's say you sit down beside someone on an airplane. The weather outdoors is miserable, causing the plane to be running late. Rain pounds against the window, adding to the sullen countenance of the person beside you.

"Great weather for ducks," he says.

"And not too intolerable for people," you add pleasantly.

He looks at you in a moment of silence. He had intended to unload all his woes, his difficulty getting to the airport, the fact he will probably miss the next two connections. But you have caught him off guard by saying something he did not intend to hear.

"The farmers around here are going to need a lot of moisture in the ground," you say, "and it'll be good to get some of that pollution washed out of the air."

That simply, you have rerouted the conversation. You have taken control.

There are, of course, innumerable ways in which you can exercise conversational control. For now, however, lets talk about those "test" questions.

Now before you use one of these questions, or a question you may develop for your own specific use, you need to do one of two things.

You must, by conversational control, open a logical area for posing the statement.

Or you must watch for a natural opening.

Frankly, I much prefer the natural opening but they don't always occur.

In either case—and I cannot over-emphasize it—you need to be intensely conscious of your dependence upon the Holy Spirit to guide you.

My "test" questions are:

> If you died today, where would you go?
> Do you know why Christ is called the Savior?
> When did you receive eternal life?
> When did you pass from death into life?
> Do you know why you are a sinner?

These may appear quite blunt to you.

They are.

But they do open the door to overt witness opportunity. That's why they must be used at an appropriate time in the conversation, unless you are singularly led of the Holy Spirit to begin with simply a blunt statement.

Now, of course, there are modifications to my "test" phrases or questions.

I was seated in a hotel coffee shop when a stranger sat down at my table. We exchanged greetings. He was a Diesel engineer from Montreal and remarked, "I wish I were in Montreal with my family. That'd be the greatest thing that could happen to me.

Here was my opportunity.

I looked at him and said, "I'd like to tell you about a great experience that came into my life."

"What was it?"

I told him.

Afterwards he said, "I wonder if I, too, could become a Christian."

That night in my hotel room he knelt and accepted Christ.

I met a young man in another hotel. Noting his southern accent, I asked, "Are you from down south of the Mason and Dixon line?"

He said, "Yes."

Here was my test question.

"What are you, a good old southern Baptist?"

"No sir, I'm a Methodist."

Here came my second test question.

"Are you a born again Methodist?"

"I'm not sure I understand what you mean."

I had the privilege of leading that young fellow to my Lord three evenings later.

These "test" questions help the soul winner determine whether or not the person to whom he speaks is spiritually hungry. I never pressure people in witnessing. I probe. If I find a man is stone cold to the gospel, I politely leave or change the subject.

Fourth: *Keep alert.*

If you meet someone and the conversation begins with that person saying, "This has been the most miserable day I've had in months," be assured that you stand on the threshold of a likely witnessing opportunity.

Or you may meet someone who grumbles, and takes God's name in vain. In the case of some Christians, profanity brings a rebuke. I never do that.

How better to say to the person, "You sound like you've had a bad day!"

He probably wants to tell you about it and, when he does, you watch for the opportunity to share your faith.

You may find someone in need of help. Never

take for granted that you just happen to be coming along the road when someone has car trouble. It could be coincidence, of course, but be alert to the possibility of a witnessing opportunity planned in advance for you by the Holy Spirit.

You might be in a hotel lobby, in some other type of waiting area, perhaps in a store, and you see someone whose facial expression indicates a troubled mind. Be alert for such people. When you see them, quietly invite the Holy Spirit to guide you. If you feel the Spirit's prompting, go to the person and offer a word of encouragement.

You might simply say, "Pardon me, I don't want to impose on you in any way. But you seem troubled about something. As a Christian, I'd be pleased to try to help you if there is any way I can."

And, foremost, keep always in mind the undergirding fact that witnessing stems from the Holy Spirit's guidance. Being alert does not simply mean watching for opportunities you can create but, much more so, keeping alert for those opportunities to which the Holy Spirit has sovreignly guided you.

I came to my office late one morning and found a salesman waiting. Being anxious to get to work, I talked to him briefly and excused him.

As he was going out of the door, however, the Holy Spirit rebuked me.

So I called him back.

He was a paper salesman. In order to talk to him until I could open up the conversation spiritually, I took him into our shipping department to show him the paper products we used. There I saw a gospel tract on the bench.

I handed the tract to him and said, "We've put these in every package leaving our plant for the past fourteen years."

He looked at it and, seeing what it was, said, "For two years I've been trying to find something in religion to hang on to."

I took him up to my office and, a short time later, he was wonderfully converted. The Holy Spirit had sent him to me that day but I almost missed him.

Oh, it's so important to keep alert. An opportunity may only have a moment's duration. But seizing the opportunity can make an eternity of difference.

Keeping alert forms a natural bridge to our next rule.

Fifth: *Look at inconveniences as potential opportunities.*

You have an important engagement, but miss a travel schedule. Or you are on your way to see someone, driving, and a detour takes you many miles off course. Always look upon such situations as part of God's plan for you. This not only softens frustration but often leads to witness opportunities.

In going to Columbus, Ohio, on business one day, I started from home in a very thick fog. When I came to a small town thirty miles away, I took a wrong turn and didn't realize my error until I had gone over twenty miles.

I stopped at the side of the road and took out a road map to see how I could correct my mistake. I needed to reach Columbus on time.

When I reached the next town, where I could make a correction and turn onto a highway which would gradually bring me back to the route I was supposed to be on, I passed a hitch hiker in his early teens. As I was about a block past him, the Holy Spirit spoke to me and said, "There is the reason I brought you through this little town.

I stopped the car and began to back up. And, as the boy saw me coming, he ran up to the car and got in.

I was listening to a religious broadcast and I said to him, "Do you know this man who is speaking on the radio?"

"No," he replied.

"Do you know the Lord Jesus Christ as your personal Savior?"

I felt the Holy Spirit had led me to this boy to witness to him and I lost no time. He was going five miles into the country to caddy at a golf course.

I told him the story of Christ and then started to ask him questions. I found he was a Sunday school boy and had basic knowledge of the gospel. But before I could bring him to a place where he realized his sin, we reached the golf course. I did not feel led to press him into a decision.

As I drove off, I lifted my heart to the Lord and prayed that the Holy Spirit would minister to him until the day he would accept Christ as his personal Saviour.

I do not know what future days will bring to this young fellow, whether he will become a preacher, missionary, or layman, but I do know this—our encounter resulted from the definite leading of the Holy Spirit. God had a purpose in the young man's life and chose me to deal with him and seal him in prayer until the day he would accept Christ into his heart and become the servant God wanted him to be.

It was downright inconvenient for me to take the wrong turn that day in the fog. I arrived late for my appointment in Columbus. But, as I said, I'm fully assured the detour occurred through the Holy Spirit's specific guidance.

We can expect this kind of leading when we consciously put our daily activity—moment by moment and, in this case, mile by mile—into His control.

For when your life is clean, consciously yielded to the Holy Spirit, and when you obey the Holy Spirit's prompting, you are always in the center of God's will—whatever the surrounding circumstances may be.

Sixth: *Remember that soul winning takes time.*

Oh, I know how some overly-zealous people go about it. The great masses of our world are living, and soon dying, without Christ, they reason. We need to go to them in haste, to sound the warning of eternal doom in the ears of everyone we can possibly confront.

Well, when the zeal is sincere, I respect such people.

But I often wonder if they are energized by the inner prompting of the Holy Spirit or by their own impulses.

Please read carefully.

We have talked about the six rules I follow in soul winning. They consist of a plan. We have talked about the importance of a plan. But, totally over-riding that importance is the fact that God has a plan for each of His individual children.

God has a plan for me.

God has a plan for you.

Not just a plan for your life but a plan for this day, for wherever you may be, whatever the circumstances.

Now it is not mine to say that God's plan for you does not involve scatter shot witnessing. I will not judge anyone. I leave that to God

But from my study of the Scriptures, and from my own years of experience, I am convinced that soul winning involves very careful, patient, considerate procedures.

The Aspostle Paul wrote, *I have planted, Apollos watered, but God gave the increase.*[8] He was talking about those with whom he had a part in bringing the Good News of the gospel of Jesus Christ.

Sometimes, in witnessing to a person, you find he has had a background in Sunday school. Or he may have had a mother who witnessed to him in childhood. Or another Christian, in the past, may have scattered the living seed of the Word of God in his mind. He may be ready right then for a decision.

On other occasions, you may have a limited amount of time. You can't bring the person to an immediate decision. You must pray much in such instances, depending upon the Holy Spirit to guide you. You may be the one responsible for seed sowing, a tremendously important responsibility.

But even when you do have ample time to talk

with a person, proceed with caution. If you push too
hard, you may try to inject your own cleverness
into the procedure. Don't ever do that! Seek always
to be keenly conscious of the Holy Spirit's guidance.

While I am witnessing to a person, I constantly
offer brief prayers to the Lord, asking Him for guidance, acknowledging my own inability to bring
someone into the awesome presence of my Creator.

Let's examine further some of the aspects involved
in this greatest of all enterprises, the business of
soul winning.

[1] Romans 12:11
[2] I Thes. 5:17.
[3] Genesis 1:2.
[4] II Peter 1:21.
[5] Luke 1:35.
[6] Psalms 126:6.
[7] Colossians 4:6.
[8] I Corinthians 3:6.

CHAPTER SIX

KNOWING THE RULES ISN'T PLAYING THE GAME

As I travel up and down the country speaking as a layman in churches, I am constantly amazed at the absence of soul winners in our congregations. Yet, at the same time, I find we have many fine Bible teachers.

We have lay teachers in some of our Sunday schools, for example, who spend hours in preparation. Visit their homes and you'll find excellent commentaries, reference books, religious magazines.

"Sunday school is much too short," people say. "We've got a fabulous teacher. He makes the Bible come alive."

I meet those teachers. On occasion I have opportunity to ask them about their personal witnessing.

Thank God, there are exceptions. But rarely do I find a teacher, however proficient he may be in the scriptures, who ever makes a really serious effort to lead a soul to the Savior.

I'm forced to the conclusion that the basic reason for fruitlessness in our lives, when it comes to soul winning, is not ignorance of the Word of God.

The basic reason is a spiritual condition.

Now please don't get me wrong. God hasn't appointed me a judge to sit in condemnation over His children. You can find too much wrong in my own glass house for me to throw stones at others.

"In this is my Father glorified," Jesus said, *"that ye bear much fruit."* [1] You'll never hear me saying that the ability to open the scriptures and effectively expound biblical truth doesn't involve being fruitful. But here's what bothers me. With multitudes all around us who do not know the Lord Jesus and with multitudes of Christians who never open their mouths in witness, dare we say the average congregation today is really fruitful?

Fruit is something living. It is something that is created. You harvest fruit. And the Bible clearly speaks of harvest as the winning of souls.

But though I find very few soul winners, I find a lot of people interested in soul winning. Talking with them, a trend seems quite evident. Many Christians want the benefits of winning souls but lack the fundamental requirement—the heart of a soul winner.

A great artist must have the heart of an artist. A great athlete must have the heart of an athlete. The word success can be spelled w-o-r-k.

You can't be spiritually lazy and win men to Christ.

Lazy Christians want to be active on committees, participate in programs, get involved in church drives. On the outside, the activity makes them look productive. All too often, however, I fear the bustle of activity consists of excuses for not getting down to the basic purpose of being a child of God.

We have talked about the rules for successful soul winning.

Now lets consider the basic human elements, the supreme personal factor which must characterize your lifestyle if you are to witness effectively.

The word is heart.

For soul winning is a heart condition.

If you are going to be a successful soul winner, you must have the heart of a soul winner, and only God —through the indwelling cleansing and impowering outflow of the Holy Spirit—can give you this heart.

To me this has such special meaning, for it strips us naked of any reason for personal boasting. You see, the heart for soul winning simply cannot be self-generated. You must receive it from the Holy Spirit. And how dare you be boastful, or take personal credit, for something given to you by God Himself?

In my opinion, pride is a kind of blasphemy.

And spiritual pride is the most dastardly of all vanity!

Now, of course, having the heart of a soul winner is only the beginning. Simply having the heart of an artist or the heart of an athlete doesn't assure success.

What "heart" does is to generate desire.

Oh, friend, if you have the desire to win men to Christ, thank God! And take courage. You possess the first single most important ingredient for success.

You can be sure Satan has a fire brigade specializing in putting out the flames of valid spiritual desire.

We need to fan those flames and add fuel to the fire.

This takes motivation.

But let's not get ahead of ourselves here. A desire, born of the Holy Spirit, has two functions. First, to make us want to win men to Christ. Second, to let the Holy Spirit cleanse us and give us the courage and guidance we need to effectively share our faith with others.

Only an intense love for Christ will initiate full surrender and bring about the infilling of the Holy Spirit. And, remember, this intense love cannot be generated within yourself. It comes from an act of commitment, prostrating yourself upon the altar of full surrender, vowing to God your mind, body and energy in total obedience.

Following such a commitment in my own experience, I determined to lay aside every encumberence and dedicate two nights a week to personal soul winning. With the encouraging cooperation of my wife, we set family plans aside so nothing would interfere. Giving glory to God, I can tell you that this disciplined regularity, with dependence upon the Holy Spirit, has caused me to see score upon score of souls, hand picked, come to accept Christ through the years.

But you must have heart—the very heart of Christ beating in your breast through the presence of the Holy Spirit.

Plus motivation.

They that sow in tears shall reap in joy, the Bible tells us, describing the heart of a soul winner. *He that goeth forth and weepeth, bearing precious seed, shall doubtless come again with rejoicing, bringing his sheaves with him.*[2]

But don't miss something very important in that verse.

True, it speaks of a weeping concern for the lost —and this we surely must have—but it also speaks of motivation.

He that soweth, the Bible says.

You can't sit in your front room reading the Bible, important as this may be, and do much sowing.

He that goeth forth, the verse also states.

Wanting to reach out to the lost isn't "going forth." Determining you will one of these days begin to witness isn't "going forth." Actually going forth is "going forth"!

We must let the Holy Spirit, who first gives us the heart of a soul winner, next give us the "muscle"— the kind of motivation which demands market place encounters by making footprints on the sidewalk of initiative.

And to me "weeping" is the key.

Maybe not actual tears—they can be artificial— but an anguished heart which simply cannot settle for complacency when men are on the road to an eternity without faith in Jesus Christ!

Show me a Christian with a weeping heart for lost souls, and I'll show you someone God is using in the manner He planned that person to be used. A weeping heart projects the convicting power of the Holy Spirit into the hearts of those to whom the Christian witnesses.

Someone once suggested it this way.

The Holy Spirit lays upon the heart of a Christian a deep concern for the lost soul of another person. This Christian begins to pray, as the burden of concern grows heavier and heavier upon his heart. When the burden grows so heavy it is almost too heavy to bear, then the Holy Spirit lifts that burden from the heart of the Christian and places it upon the one for whom the Christian has been praying. The burden now becomes a burden of conviction for sin, causing the lost one to turn to Christ.

I can't vouch for the theology of that beautiful concept. But I do know it takes a burden on your heart to cause you to witness and, when you do, to bring conviction to the hearts of those to whom you relate. You can't casually talk to people about Christ the way you talk to them about the weather.

It deeply concerns me today to see the church trying to win souls through programs and entertainment. The command is to go, not to attract people to our churches in the hope they will come and find salvation. An effective soul winner must shake himself free from much of the machinery of the church, if he is going to find time to contact the lost.

The sinner is lost, you know, as helpless as someone lost in a vast jungle. He doesn't know where he is, where to go to get out of his plight.

You and I must go to him, not wait for him to come to us!

And it isn't as difficult as you might think.

Not by might, nor by power, but by my Spirit, saith the Lord of Hosts.[3] The hardest part in becoming a soul winner is to learn that it is not by schemes, programs, talent display, but by putting ourselves obediently into the Holy Spirit's control.

Since the Lord laid it upon my heart to do soul winning many years ago, I have had only one problem—yielding and letting Him do the work through me. I'm a fairly resourceful person and like to do things my own way. But as I depend more upon the Holy Spirit, I see more and more that I serve only as the glove on the hand that does the work.

This struck me forcefully one evening, early in my experience in soul winning, as I visited the home of a young couple who had attended our church for almost a year. Morally, you would say they truly exemplified Christian virtues. Actually, I had come on a social call. But, as we sat talking, I felt strongly impressed that they were not Christians.

So I asked, "How long have you people been Christians?"

To which the young wife quickly replied. "Oh, we aren't Christians."

"Do you want to be?" I asked.

"Yes," she replied, glancing at her husband whose eyes spoke silent approval. "We're tired of pretending."

Bringing them to the Savior was like picking beautiful ripe fruit!

You see, winning them was not something I did. I took them to be Christians. But I had rerouted my life, so that I consciously permitted the Holy Spirit to guide me and use me in any circumstance. Thus, visiting in their home, the Holy Spirit gave me the strong impression of their lostness.

Not by might, nor by power, but by my Spirit, saith the Lord of hosts.

Now, of course, the most effective soul winner will face obstacles. When you face them, keep in mind that magnificant Bible verse—a question with a self-contained answer: *Is anything too hard for the Lord?*[4]

Returning from South America a few years ago, I chatted with a fellow passenger as we cleared immigration at San Juan. We talked casually and although, of course, I would have liked to have shared my faith with him, there was no opportunity to do so.

I put the matter from my mind.

But when we left San Juan, heading homeward, I recognized the man sitting on the opposite side of the plane about five rows away from us.

Juanita and I rode in the tourist section, and every seat was taken.

"There is a soul going out into eternity without Christ, unless you speak to him." Almost like an audible voice, the words went through my mind.

"But Lord," I prayed silently, "it would be impossible to get over to him. He is sitting by the window, and there are two people between him and the aisle."

"If you don't speak to him about Christ," the voice seemed to continue, "perhaps no one ever will."

Still I hesitated.

Then an awesome sense of my disobedience came over me. *Grieve not the Holy Spirit,*[5] the Bible admonishes us.

So I prayed, "Lord, if you'll make it possible for me to do so, I will witness to that man."

Immediately, the pilot came onto the intercom and announced an island beneath us. The gentleman arose, worked his way to the aisle, and went to look at a map of the Carribean posted in the galley area. There were no stewardesses, no passengers in the galley area, just this man.

Quickly, I arose and went to him.

"Nice to see you again," I said.

He looked at me, smiled warmly in remembrance of our previous, brief conversation.

"I have been praying for you," I said quietly. "May I talk to you about some spiritual things?"

He seemed neither surprised nor offended at my direct approach. Instead, he nodded.

My wife left her seat, so the man and I could spend time together. After an hour with an open Bible, he prayed and asked Jesus to come into his life.

It was all so easy, that when I got home I wrote and asked him if he really did accept Christ that day. What a joy to get his answer, vigorously affirming that he had!

Do you see the pattern?

There are no happenstances with the Christian,

no casual encounters. The Holy Spirit led me to make an initial acquaintance with this man, going through immigration in San Juan. For, of course, the Holy Spirit knew we would again be travelling on the same plane!

The Holy Spirit will guide you to those to whom He has prepared for witness. You must not fail to obey.[6]

You see, the key to soul winning is a matter of priority—your recognizing the Holy Spirit's priority over you as an instrument of witness. No wonder the Holy Spirit is grieved when Christians fail to witness. The Holy Spirit cannot approach men except through a human instrument. When a Christian refuses to be that instrument, and people who could be won to Christ go unreached, how great must be the anguish to the heart of our Lord.

Priorities!

Have you settled that word in your Christian life?

Seek ye first the kingdom of God and his righteousness, the Bible counsels, *and all these things shall be added unto you.*[7]

Do you do it?

In everything?

When you go to the drugstore, are you going only for a selfish reason, to buy a tube of toothpaste, or are you alert for the possibility that the Holy Spirit might have led you for a particular need in someone's life?

How about it when you go to the filling station? Are you seeking a selfish reason, gasoline for your car? What if the attendant has a hungry heart and today would be ready to receive a testimony from you?

I was in Lincoln, Nebraska, and went downtown to purchase a gift for my wife. The lady who waited for me was so helpful, I kidded her and said, "I don't give everybody my picture, but I want to give you a copy of my testimony."

Briefly, I talked to her about the Lord, then gave her a little pamphlet with my picture and testimony.

Several weeks later, she wrote to the address on the pamphlet and told me that, from reading that testimony, she had given her heart to Christ.

My wife and I ate in a restaurant in Spokane, Washington. I left a copy of the testimony at the table, with a note of thanks to the waitress for having been so helpful.

Several weeks later, we received a letter in which she wrote, "It was no accident you ate in my restaurant. I was a backslidden Christian. But as I began to read your testimony, God spoke to me, and I went to a room in the back of the restaurant, got on my knees and came back to Christ."

In everything . . . yes, everything . . . seek first the kingdom of God and you will begin to see fruit in your life.

The supreme objective of every Christian should be to glorify Christ.

And how can you best glorify Him?

Jesus said, *"Herein is my Father glorified that ye bear much fruit; so shall ye be my diciples."* [8]

Every Christian is "ordained" [9] to go and bring forth fruit.

Personal soul winning was the living heart of the early church. As personal workers, the disciples went out—John here, Peter there, Phillip yonder. Ordinary Christian laymen, just like you, they carried the witness of Christ from city to city and from village to village and from house to house.

And, as a result, the Lord added to the church daily [10] the results of this personal soul winning effort.

You and I can be part of that triumphant ministry yet today!

Why not?

[1] John 15:8.
[2] Psalm 126:5-6.
[3] Zachariah 4:6.
[4] Genesis 18:4.
[5] Ephesians 4:30.
[6] I Samuel 12:22.
[7] Matthew 6:33.
[8] John 15:8.
[9] John 15:16.
[10] Acts 2:46.

CHAPTER SEVEN
OBEDIENCE PLUS INITIATIVE EQUALS RESULTS

The problem with many Christians is that they see the church building as the terminal point in soul winning effort.

Instead, the church should serve as a launching pad!

I don't take the extreme view of some, who believe the church edifice should serve solely as a center for worship and teaching. We still have many churches where, especially at the Sunday night service, pastors effectively preach the Gospel and lost souls, invited to church by concerned neighbors and friends, make public professions of salvation through Jesus Christ.

May such pastors and churches increase!

In my frequent travels across North America, I am privileged to visit many such churches, to meet the pastors. But I have yet to find a pastor, however effective he may be in pulpit evangelism, who does not yearn to see his people reach out across the community in personal soul winning.

And, thank God, sometimes they do. So that a pastor and congregation team together—some people finding Christ in the sanctuary, in other cases the harvest taking place out in homes or shops or offices of the secular city.

As I stated earlier, however, all too few Christians today have any kind of story to tell when it comes to reaching others for Christ through their own specific efforts. This tragedy is compounded by the fact that, in addition to not reaching out to the unchurched with the gospel, few Christians ever try to follow through in trying to win those lost souls who do come occasionally to worship services. Such people surely demonstrate some kind of interest in the gospel, if they willingly attend an evangelical church. When they do come, the good seed of God's word is sown in their hearts.

So why not follow through with them?

But that is the pastor's job, you hear people say. That's why he goes to the door and greets people as they go by. True enough, many a soul winning pastor takes his cue from the hunger he sees in the eye of someone with whom he shakes hands at the conclusion of a service.

But soul winning is the prime responsibility of us laymen. The pastor, by the very definition of his title, serves as the shepherd of the sheep. He teaches, helps new converts come to grips with the Word of God. He stands as a guardian over our lives, helping us when we falter, guiding us when we stray.

My own conviction is that, when he witnesses on a one-to-one basis, the pastor functions the same as a layman. You don't expound the gospel when you witness. You proclaim the gospel. You serve, beautifully and uniquely, as the instrument through whom the Holy Spirit flows out to those in need of redeeming love.

But even the pastor, eager though he may be to meet the spiritual needs of all who hear his message, cannot possibly reach everyone who darkens the church's door. Laymen must share the load.

You shall be witnesses unto me,[1] the Lord Jesus said. That includes clergymen, to be sure. But it also includes deacons and ushers, choir members and Sunday school teachers. It includes people in the pews, who know and love the Savior.

It includes doctors, lawyers, teachers, stenographers, bus drivers, filling station attendants, students, clerks, housewives, welders, salesmen, lathe operators, medical technicians, automotive mechanics, janitors, pilots, taxi drivers, retired people.

It includes you!

I wonder how many children have attended Sunday school in evangelical churches without anyone, including the teacher and the superintendent, ever making an effort to reach them for Christ. I wonder how many parents have come to Christmas programs, to Rally Day activities, to other special events in the church, and though Christians have been friendly to them, no one ever made an effort to win them.

Being a member of a church is a responsibility, a sacred trust!

I often look at the church bulletin, when I am gone weekends on speaking engagements, and like to read some of the slogans that appear. I think the one I like best is: *Come in to worship. Go out to serve.*

Serve?

What does that mean?

Well, I do not deny but what service has many ramifications. But I must bluntly insist that, as I understand my Bible, the foremost responsibility in service is to convey the gospel of Jesus Christ, as you hear it proclaimed in your church, to the unchurched out in your community and across your world!

But let's get back to these people who do attend your church, even though infrequently, but who do not know Christ as Savior. As I write these words, I'm praying the Holy Spirit will prick your conscience. And I pray that next Sunday—and the next and the next—when you see such people in your church, you will be gripped with a keen sense of responsibility.

I mentioned earlier my experiences as a Sunday school superintendent. Thank God for the good Sunday school staff people we have in so many of our churches. It's amazing how much is often accomplished in those miserly forty minutes or so once a week, in comparison to the thirty hours and more spent in public schools. But always remember, friend, teaching or administering a Sunday school must never serve as your cop out for neglecting personal soul winning!

We had a Sunday school contest in our church

back in those years when I served as superintendent, and someone invited a meat salesman to attend our adult class. He accepted the invitation, came with his wife, liked our congregation, and so began to attend regularly. I, of course, was pleased to see a new family in the congregation as a result of my efforts in the contest.

Some months passed. The man who invited this couple came to me and said, "That family puzzles me. They look like Christians. They act like Christians. They show a lot of interest in spiritual things. But there's something that I just can't put my finger on."

So I called the young couple, said I'd like to get better acquainted, and asked if I could come over some night. This worked out beautifully, of course, with my role as Sunday school superintendent.

They responded most cordially, and we set a night for getting together.

My job was to find out whether or not they were Christians. The best way to do this, of course, was to ask.

The wife seemed the most responsive, so I said, "How long have you people been born again Christians?"

"Oh, Mr. Tam, we're not born again Christians," the lady replied. I still remember the touch of anguish in her voice.

"Would you like to be?" I asked.

"More than anything else in the world," she said. She glanced to her husband. "As you've noticed, we attend Sunday evenings quite regularly. When my

91

husband is gone—he travels as a salesman—I come alone. When your pastor gives the invitation to come forward at the altar, why, the very thought of leaving my seat and walking in front of all those people almost gives me a nervous breakdown. I stand there and tremble, wanting to respond, but I just can't."

"Does that wooden altar at the front of the church give anyone redemption?" I asked.

"No," she said, "only Jesus Christ can do that."

"Do you believe that Jesus Christ is omnipresent? That He is everywhere?"

"Oh, yes!"

"Then, that being true, He is right here in your home tonight, isn't He?"

"Why, yes," she said, the glow of awareness coming to her eyes.

"So if you are ready," I said tactfully, "you could give your heart to Christ right now."

She turned to her husband. He was not quite ready. So I asked if I might explain some of the verses in the scripture which had to do with receiving Christ. To this he was agreeable.

And, no more than a half hour later, this couple—who looked like Christians, acted like Christians, showed interest in spiritual things—received Jesus Christ as their Savior.

Take a good look at those people in your church next Sunday. Let the Holy Spirit remind you it isn't enough to be able to look like Christians. Doesn't the Bible speak of *tares among the wheat?* [2]

Now, of course, you don't promptly go up to every

person whose salvation you may question and begin witnessing. First you must pray! Remind God continually, and particularly when you are in the presence of people of whose spiritual condition you are not sure, that you are available to serve as the Holy Spirit's instrument in outreach to the lost. The Holy Spirit will guide you. It will thrill you to sense His sure directions, as your mind is put into his Master-control and you sense His leading in relating to others.

It is when you clearly sense this leading that you must exert initiative. To do otherwise means just one thing—disobedience.

And disobedience is sin!

Christians who are quick to point out the faults of others, who do not themselves endeavor to win souls to Christ, need to be reminded that the greatest sin a man can commit is to stand as the barrier between someone and eternal salvation. You become such a barrier when you refuse to function as the Holy Spirit's voice in witness!

What a folly to criticize any Christian. But ever so much greater the folly when Christians sit in judgment but, in their refusal to witness, are themselves under the greatest guilt.

Listen, Christian, adultery—heinous as it may be —is no greater sin in God's sight than refusing to let the Holy Spirit lead us into the harvest of lost souls!

Never, never forget that!

I cannot overemphasize the importance of seeking the Holy Spirit's guidance.

Why not begin with some of those visitors at your

church, in addition to people you may meet at work? Designate at least one night a week for soul winning. After prayer, pick three prospects, and start out. Start at least by seven o'clock, because the first may not be at home.

If a prospect does not appear responsive after your second or third call, take him off your list. But keep him on your prayer list, because the Holy Spirit may need to further prepare him for the time of harvest.

Many soul winners fail and become discouraged by dealing with people who are not interested but too polite to say so.

I particularly remember Betty and Chuck, a young couple who were satisfied with simply being religious. I called on them several times. They welcomed me into their home, listened attentively, but gave no indication of personal need.

So I stopped calling.

But I continued praying for them.

A year later, Betty and Chuck fell victims of a broken home.

They had two small children and Betty, realizing her need, called me since I had shown interest in her and her husband a year before.

And, I'm convinced, because I never stopped praying for them!

With one of the elders of our church to help me, we got the two parents together. The seed had had many months to germinate in their hearts. Now, because of what had happened in their marriage, they recognized their spiritual need, that simply being religious would not suffice.

That night they both accepted Christ. Three days later they buried their pride, reestablished their home, this time on Christ.

So never be discouraged in your soul winning efforts. Not if you are sure the Holy Spirit is guiding you. Many times you must make the contacts, then prayerfully wait as the Holy Spirit prepares the prospect for the miracle of new birth.

Oh, I cannot over emphasize the need for the Holy Spirit's guidance. Of course, as we've already seen, you must exert initiative. But that initiative stems from the Holy Spirit's prompting, not from your own energy and ingenuity.

And when you witness to people, don't pressure. The Holy Spirit, not you, is the one who will succeed. When you are privileged to bring people to Christ, be careful of pride. You aren't a hunter, exhibiting game trophies. You are an instrument, a vehicle, a channel.

Always remember that!

So success is not your prime concern. Of course, you want to succeed. You must realize that failure just could be because of your unwillingness to be fully led by the Holy Spirit, because you try to take things into your own hands. That's why, when you witness, you need such a keen perception, a child's faith in expecting and anticipating the Holy Spirit's sure direction.

And the Holy Spirit will direct you, if you'll permit Him to!

I realize that, if you and I were sitting face to face —and how I wish we were—you might say to me,

"But, Mr. Tam, you just don't realize my situation, my limitations?"

No, I don't, and you may have very legitimate limitations. But God knows. And, regardless of your limitations, your heavenly Father wants you to be one of His harvesters!

Don't let that fact alarm you, cause you to have a guilt complex. Let it be a cause for rejoicing.

Let's look at that word guilt a moment.

When I say unto the wicked, Thou shalt surely die; and thou givest him not warning, nor speakest to warn the wicked from his wicked way, to save his life, the same wicked man shall die in his iniquity; but his blood will I require at thine hand. Yet if thou warn the wicked, and he turns not from his wicked way, he shall die in his iniquity; but thou hast delivered thy soul.[3]

Those awesome words, so clearly speaking out about obedience and disobedience in witnessing, strike with the thrust of a dagger. They terrify many Christians.

And rightly so.

But those words only state the terrifying importance of witness. They should not drive us to guilt.

Unless, of course, we're guilty.

Maybe you swelter under a guilt complex.

If so, please pay very close attention.

Permit guilt to be your motivation in witnessing, and you can't expect God to bless you. Because, you see, you will be witnessing by your own strength. You will be doing penance, as it were, witnessing because you fear the judgment of having some sinner's blood on your hands.

Ah, no, that's not the way!

Not at all!

If you feel guilt, come to the God who loves you. Confess your sins of negligence, coldness, whatever may have kept you from witnessing. By a solemn act of your faith, put yourself completely into the Holy Spirit's control.

Then—you must understand this!—you witness by the Holy Spirit's guidance, with the courage and wisdom He gives, and not in your own strength and wisdom.

If you face other problems in witnessing, such as fear or personal limitations or whatever, put that into the Holy Spirit's control, too.

Whenever I meet people who talk about the barriers they face in witnessing, I like to tell about the farmer's wife who led me to Christ.

As a teenager, I tried my hand at all kinds of selling. I would literally scour the magazines which came to our home, sending in for free samples and asking for a sales kit when I saw some product I thought I could sell. In my trusty Ford I drove from farmstead to farmstead across our community, endeavoring to peddle my wares.

One day I stopped at a farmhouse.

It was the heart of the depression, money scarce, but the woman of the house, Mrs. George Long, not only met me pleasantly at the door, listened attentively to my sales pitch, but made a couple of purchases. Then she drew me into a conversation, about conditions in the country at first. However, I could see she was moving toward a religious subject and grew uneasy.

So I got up to go.

"Just a moment," Mrs. Long said. "Please sit down."

I complied.

"I gave you time to tell me about the things you have to sell," she said. "Now maybe you would be willing to listen to my presentation."

I say Mrs. Long led me to Christ. Actually, I came to Christ at the Sunday evening service of our church, which I had previously attended with a casual take-it-or-leave-it attitude.

But the witness of that dear lady burned conviction upon my heart. She prayed hours for me, believed the seed sown in my heart would bring fruit.

Whereas I had been casual before about spiritual things, after Mrs. Long's witness the need of my soul took precedence in my thoughts. I went to sleep thinking about my spiritual condition. I awakened thinking about it. I was miserable.

Until that liberating, transforming moment at the altar of our church!

Because I was the first one in our family converted, I used to go back to Mrs. Long's home frequently for guidance. She became like a spiritual mother to me.

One day she said, "Stanley, do you wonder why I witnessed to you the day you came to my farmhouse?"

Then she told me the story.

There came a time in her Christian life when she wanted to win souls more than anything else in the world. But here she was far out in the country on a farm, in the heart of the depression, with no extra money to buy gasoline, farmhouses too far apart for her to walk, especially with small children keeping her at home.

Yet the burden for soul winning grew heavier and heavier upon her heart, until one day she went into her bedroom and knelt and cried out, "God, I can't go into town, I can't go door to door, but I must win souls! Please, God, make my front room my church. You bring lost souls to my door."

God answered that prayer. I was the seventh soul she had won to Christ, each of whom had come to her door guided by the Holy Spirit in answer to her prayer.

Too timid to go door to door in witnessing?

Then pray that lost souls will come to you.

For if you honestly seek guidance of the Holy Spirit upon your life, if you will be obedient to His guidance, you will be led to those who need to know your Savior!

But, remember, obedience is just one sum in the total quotient. When you are obedient, the Holy Spirit will respond with guidance. And when you sense the Holy Spirit's guidance, you must exert initiative.

The result is sure success!

[1] Acts 1:8.
[2] Matthew 13:25.

CHAPTER EIGHT
GOD NEVER MAKES DUPLICATES

If He blueprinted creation, so no two snowflakes ever appear in the same form, you can be sure God doesn't make duplicate people.

So, since all people are different, no two Christians witness in quite the same manner. Nor are any two witnessing situations ever identical. For every human being consists of a separate, unique entity unto himself.

In spite of the reticence of my early years, I now love to meet people. The Holy Spirit transformed a shy farmboy into a genuinely gregarious human being.

I like to watch people when I travel, watch them in stores, restaurants, hotels. Some go about their business all but unmindful of anyone else. Others, on the contrary, almost immediately strike up a conversation when someone crosses their paths or sits beside them.

It's good to see people in relaxed, friendly conversation.

Yet, because of the joy I have found in witnessing, a touch of sadness comes to my heart when I hear Christians chatting about politics, the weather, last Saturday's ball game.

Because, you see, no human encounter can equal the rewarding inner satisfaction of those times when one meets a stranger, finds out something about him, then shares the Lord Jesus Christ with him.

Now, of course, I'm not opposed to casual conversation in its place. I enjoy pleasant discussions, very much. But I also know there won't be any weather reports in heaven, no political campaigns or elections, and I fear some Christians will find themselves ill prepared for eternal bliss because they majored in too many minors here on earth. I wonder, too, how many of God's children will get to Heaven—*where every man's work shall be made manifest; for the day shall declare it, for it shall be revealed by fire; and the fire shall test every man's work of what sort it is.*[1]—and look back across the expanse of a lifetime and realize how many, many times they faced open doors to witness which they deliberately closed through carelessness or disobedience.

As I say, I try to be a good conversationalist. I chat with people about affairs of the day. We Christians don't live in ivory towers but right here on the troubled surface of planet earth. But I can tell you that I make it my avowed goal to begin every conversation with a stranger, or with someone whom I strongly suspect to be outside of Christ, by breathing a silent prayer in which I consciously put myself into the control of the Holy Spirit and depend upon

Him to open up opportunities for sharing my faith.

You've doubtless read or heard it said that the best conversationalist is a good listener.

True.

And so apropos in soul winning!

Because, as I said, since God makes no two people alike, the spiritual needs of people assume unlimited variety. So how can you best relate to a lost soul, if you don't first try to find out who he is, what his problems are, what he is thinking, what he longs for?

You can't get that information by doing all the talking.

You've got to listen.

Dr. Walter Wilson, one of the most successful soul winners of all time, said, "The best way to open a conversation is to ask a question. It's like punching a hole in the bottom of a barrel. You can just sit back and let the person do all the talking. Let the barrel empty itself and, when it is empty, you can put something in."

Also, since religion is such a mute subject with so many people, you often need to establish rapport before you can introduce your faith. Beyond that, you need to know the person's background. Does he attend church? Is he Catholic, Protestant, Jewish?

Or perhaps nothing?

Never approach a Catholic on the same basis you would a Jew. Nor do you witness to a lost church going person on the same basis as one who never darkens a sanctuary.

My approach is to strike up a conversation, then carefully listen as the person talks. I may find a natural opening for witness. Or I may make mental note of several things the person says, using them later when I have opportunity to introduce life's most important subject.

A missionary from one of the Muslim tribal areas tells that preaching is an impossibility on his field. Make a statement about anything, and by tradition someone must respond—often in an argumentative vein, even though he agrees with your premise. To reach such people, the missionary relates, he can only enter into conversation, waiting for specific moments when the subject matter lends itself to introducing salient aspects of the Christian faith.

As I suggested before, I find the use of questions extremely helpful in witnessing.

Get a person talking about his family, his business, his community, and you are sure to have numerous opportunities to introduce a question about his church relationships, his spiritual interests.

Ken Anderson, who is assisting me in writing this book, has an approach which both he and his wife use. They produce Christian films, among them the dramatized motion picture on my own personal testimony. So, when striking up a conversation, they try to move the subject into the area of business. Invariably, they will be asked what sort of business they are in.

"We make motion pictures," is always the answer.

Virtually without exception, the person wants to know what kind of motion pictures.

"We produce films primarily for the evangelical church," is the reply. By this time the door is wide open for witness opportunities.

In my own case, my wife Juanita and I have literally made God our business partner. So I, too, can use the "what sort of business are you in?" approach to opening the door to opportunity.

But you don't need this kind of natural entre, of course.

In fact, I more often try to simply invade the flow of conversation with a direct approach to spiritual things. For I find that, though most people try to put up a pleasant front, deep down inside they have great spiritual need.

So, frequently, I will simply begin the question by asking, "Are you interested in spiritual things?"

The person may ask, "What do you mean?"

A logical question, with occult phenomena so prevelant these days, foreign *gurus* gaining front page publicity in our country.

So my next question is likely to be, "Are you interested in the kind of spiritual experiences the Bible talks about?"

Only rarely do I get a negative response. The answer is usually a simple, "Yes."

So I ask, "Have you ever thought about becoming a Christian?"

Note that I do not ask, "Are you a Christian?" Ask this of many people, especially if they attend church on occasion, and you will likely get a positive response. So I ask whether they have ever thought of becoming a Christian. It puts the person on the defensive.

"Well," he will probably respond, "I think I am a Christian."

So, casually, but with intense concern, I continue

the interrogation with, "If someone were to ask you what a Christian is, what would you answer?"

"Oh," people often say, "a Christian is someone who goes to church on Sunday."

"Christians surely should go to church on Sunday," you agree, "But what is a Christian?"

"I suppose one who keeps the Ten Commandments.

"A Christian surely should keep the Ten Commandments. But what is a Christian?"

"Well, he treats his neighbor right, doesn't steal, lie."

To this I agree, but continue asking the question. "What is a Christian?"

Finally the person will say, "You tell me what you think a Christian is."

Then, of course, I have the golden opportunity to say, "I don't need to tell you what I think a Christian is, I can tell you what I *know* a Christian is. Because my definition is based on the Bible."

It is vitally important to get down to bedrock biblical principles in witnessing. Never be content to talk around the subject of what it really means to know Christ. The Apostle Paul wrote, *"I am determined not to know anything among you, save Jesus Christ, and Him crucified."* [2]

Let that be your objective. Many opportunities can be missed if we permit ourselves to be diverted by what seems to indicate that the person to whom we are talking is a Christian.

I spoke to a men's group in a community one time. The local newspaper picked it up, doing a small feature on how God became Senior Partner in our business. As a result I received a letter from a lawyer several weeks later saying he used to live in that town where I had spoken and still took the hometown paper. He was intrigued by my philosophy of making God our Senior Partner, wanted to do this himself, and asked me for details.

Now one might logically assume that no one would write such a letter unless he had a genuine experience in Christ himself. But when we let the Holy Spirit be our guide, we don't assume anything. We depend upon Him to give us careful discernment in every opportunity.

I wrote to this lawyer, gave him the details of our business, but then felt strongly constrained to add an emphasis that the most important thing was to know Christ as personal Savior. To make sure he understood, I outlined the plan of Salvation.

No sooner had he received my letter than he called me long distance, some three hundred miles, and said, "Can I see you tomorrow? I've got to talk to you."

The Holy Spirit used my letter to prick his heart with conviction and the next day in my office he accepted Christ as his personal savior. In the first two years of his Christian life, he pointed eighteen others to the Savior. He agreed he picked some of them as green fruit and it spoiled, but he quickly showed evidence that the Holy Spirit within us is the true soul winner.

In the next chapter, I'd like us to consider the "green fruit" situation a bit more.

For now, I'd like to share with you some other aspects of the use of questions in witnessing.

Three things hinder many Christians from launching a soul winning ministry—the fear of man, lack of a plan, the feeling of being ill at ease. Believe me, in my early shy attempts, all of these plagued my efforts.

But, avowedly determined to witness, I designed a poll for use on trains, busses, planes, house to house, in hotel lobbies, wherever I might be.

I would simply say to a stranger, "Would you do me a favor? I'm taking a poll; you know, like the Gallup poll. Will you give me your opinion on five questions?"

Rarely did anyone ever turn me down.

My questions were:

1. Do you believe in life after death?
2. Do you believe the Bible to be the inspired word of God?
3. Do you think the Bible presents Jesus Christ as the Savior?
4. What do you think the Bible considers the greatest sin a man can commit?
5. Romans 3:23 says; *All have sinned and come short of the glory of God.* How do you think mankind can be redeemed?

I had these printed, so I could place them in front of the person. I could write a chapter on some of the spiritually misguided responses I received!

But the questionnaire established rapport, introduced the subject of spiritual things, again and again opened the door of opportunity.

When opportunity came, I would simply say, "I've had a great experience in my life. I wonder if I might take a minute to tell you what it was?"

With the person's consent, I gave my testimony, leaving out unnecessary details, getting right to the point.

You may want to use this kind of questionnaire yourself. You are free to do so. Or you may want to make up questions of your own. Such a poll, I have found, eliminates many barriers and gives you a plan. It gives you a chance to: 1. Ask questions. 2. Give your testimony. 3. Talk to the person about his soul.

And, of course, as you converse, you begin to determine what sort of person you are addressing. The various hues of his background, his thought patterns, his basic lifestyle come into view.

You'll discover again and again how true it is that God never makes duplicates. Yet, and this is so much the wonder of it, you will also discover how appropriate the Gospel and the teaching of the Bible are to every man's need.

But though not only does one never find two identical human beings on this earth, the opposite swing of the pendulum is that many many people tend to have varying extremes of opinion and attitude. Yet I'm of the opinion people may be twenty percent different due to background and culture, but they are eighty percent the same as human beings.

So, wrapping up this chapter, I'd like to suggest a list of universal do's and don'ts which I have found so very helpful in my soul winning efforts.

Do . . .

Speak with authority. Use such expressions as "God says," or "The Bible says."

Ask warmly human questions. Be genuinely interested in the person. The Holy Spirit will give you this kind of concern. Encourage the one to whom you speak to unload his heart.

Pray constantly for wisdom. Isn't it wonderful to know that God can read our thoughts, thus always hear our silent prayers?

Be sure you have sweet breath. Halitosis and the gospel don't mix!

Show a deep sense of confidence. Be absolutely sure of your own personal experience, and the total reliability of the Word of God.

Put the person with whom you speak at ease as quickly as you can. If you see him becoming tense, invite the Holy Spirit to guide your conversation so you can ease his tension.

Don't embarrass anyone. If you are in a public place, speak quietly. If you want to use your Bible in referring to a passage of Scripture, ask first if it is alright to do so.

In making house calls, remember a man's home is his castle. You must come as a visitor, a friend, not an intruder.

Be a good listener. You must sound out a man's mind and heart before you can help him.

Be enthusiastic. Be sure your enthusiasm is genuine. Keep the enthusiasm at a low, believable pitch, but keep it obvious.

Tell yourself, "Here is a person with an eternal soul. I must help this person find Christ."

Give your testimony, it is the best way to present the plan of salvation.

Seek a decision as early as possible.

Have a definite plan.

Whenever possible, avoid trying to witness to too many people at one time. The individual person-to-person approach is always best.

Don't . . .

Don't argue. If you win an argument, you have probably lost your prospect!

Don't preach. Share, witness, converse.

Don't talk boastfully.

Don't attempt to be familiar. You represent the King of Kings. Be warm, open, believable, but declare the eternal message with dignity.

Don't point your finger at someone's face.

Don't interrupt a person while he is talking, lest you offend him. Remember, he may say something which will give you a new area of opportunity in witnessing.

Don't talk about your petty grievances.

111

Don't criticize someone else's church or religious beliefs.

Don't tell long stories or illustrations. Watch the person's eyes. They will tell you whether he is following you or if his mind is beginning to drift.

Don't be in a hurry.

Don't force, beg or coax.

Follow the above suggestions, give careful heed to the Holy Spirit's directions, and a fascinating by product will emerge in your experience. You'll become effective in sharing your faith, and that's most important, but you will also increasingly mature as a person.

Witnessing to people is a high echelon endeavor. How tragic to see any Christian cheapen the gospel by fanatic witness. As I said before, you represent the King of Kings, the Lord of Lords.

So anticipate growth in your own life, growth and enrichment, as you share your faith with others.

[1] I Corinthians 3:13.
[2] I Corinthians 2:2.

CHAPTER NINE

DON'T TRY TO PICK GREEN APPLES

Charles Finney had a technique for determining whether a lost person, to whom he witnessed, was an awakened sinner or a convicted sinner.

He determined an awakened sinner, with this type of dialogue. "If you died right now," Finney asked, "where would you go?"

To this the person might say, "I don't know."

"Would you go to hell?" Finney then asked.

"No, I don't think God, being a God of love, would send anyone to hell."

"Would you go to heaven?"

"No, I'm not good enough to go to heaven."

Such a person, Finney said, is an awakened sinner. He knows he has a spiritual need but is not convinced he is lost. If you asked him to make a decision, you would pick green fruit and it would spoil.

Dialogue with a convicted sinner, Finney discovered, runs something like this.

"If you died right now, where would you go?"

To this the convicted sinner would respond, "There is no question. I'd go straight to hell."

Such a person is already "half-converted," in a sense, and you can proceed to ask him to make a decision.

When I encounter such a person, I ask him if he is prepared to get off the throne of his life and let Christ reign there as Lord and Savior.

When it is convenient to do so, I ask a person to kneel for prayer. Now, of course, there is no specific spiritual virtue in kneeling. Some Christians have gotten away from it entirely. But I find it helpful to assume a posture which one otherwise never uses. Kneeling, of course, dates back to the times when people prostrated themselves before a higher being, such as a Lord or a King.

That's just what Jesus wants to be in our lives—Lord and King!

Please do not build up a sense of inadequacy in this matter of knowing when spiritual fruit is ready for the picking and when people should not be pushed into a decision. There's no formula. Of course, the more experienced you become in witnessing, the more perceptive you'll become.

But, as we're trying to stress in this book, the important thing is to become receptive to the Holy Spirit's guidance. When your human mind is Master-controlled by the Holy Spirit, you'll have perceptiveness you never imagined possible!

I respect the medical profession, skilled diagnostics, expert surgery. But I wouldn't trade places with the most proficient MD on earth, not for one moment, if it meant exchanging that skill for my experience as a soul winner. Nothing anywhere can equal the joy of diagnosing, through the wisdom available in the Holy Spirit, the need in a man's heart and then, applying the scalpel of the Word of God,[1] to isolate his sin and lay his heart open to the redeeming inflow of God's marvelous grace.

But once again I repeat, the Holy Spirit within us is the soul winner, the one who must reveal the contacts, the one who gathers the harvest.

Our concern must be to make sure we are Master-controlled by Him!

One night, shortly after the publication of the book on my testimony and experiences, I was about to leave my office for the day. Then our receptionist called to tell me a businessman up front wanted to talk to me. So I went to him.

"I've just read your book," he said, "and I have several questions I'd like to ask you."

From the texture of his questions, I surmised he was not a Christian. To be completely sure, I asked him if he believed in hell.

"No," he responded bluntly, "nor do I believe I'm a sinner, as you indicate in your book."

"My heart goes out to you," I said warmly, "If you're not a sinner, there's not much God can do for you, because Christ only died for sinners on the cross."

This stopped him with a question left limp on his tongue.

I waited a moment. Silence can be so golden at a time like this! Then I asked him if we might talk further and, when he assented, invited him to my office.

"May I show you something in the Bible?" I asked.

"Sure," he said.

So I opened to the sixteenth chapter of Luke and read to him about the rich man and Lazarus.

"What does it mean here," I asked, "when it says the rich man died and was buried?"

"They had a funeral for him."

So I read on, *"In hell he lifted up his eyes, being in torment, and seeth Abraham afar off, and Lazarus in his bosom."*

"Look," I continued, turning from the Bible momentarily. "Although this man had a funeral, he was still alive and had all his faculties. He could see, feel, talk, remember."

My visitor was on guard, half-skeptical, but interested.

Silently imploring the Holy Spirit's guidance, I read on. I felt strongly directed to the twentieth chapter of Revelation.

"Here the Bible describes that day when all mankind will stand before the Lord Jesus Christ." I said, "seeing Him not as Savior but as Judge." Then I read, *"And I saw the dead, small and great, stand before God, and the books were opened; and another book was opened, which is the Book of Life. And the dead were judged out of those things which were written in the books, according to their works. And the sea gave up the dead that were in it, and death and Hades delivered up the dead that were in them; and they were judged every man according*

*to their works . . . and whosoever was not found
written in the book of life was cast into the lake of
fire."* [2]

I hesitated.

In anguish, my heart cried out to God for wisdom,
for that clear and quiet assurance of being in his
will. No drama, no ersatz tension on television or in
the theater can equal the sheer awe of seeing a man,
who has lived his life contesting the authority of the
scriptures, brought to a place where he begins to
cower under the impact of the living Truth.

I don't find it necessary to defend the Bible. Oh,
I know, archeological discoveries and the like have
had a tremendous impact upon people who question
the Word of God. But I see the Bible as its own
defense, *for the word of God is living, and powerful,
and sharper than any two-edged sword.* [3]

As the silence lengthened, I said quietly, trying to
be helpfully informative rather than pushing my
position, "Do you know there is more scripture in
the Bible about hell than there is about heaven."

Just then he winced. "I've got a pain in my side."
he said, "I've had it since I was a kid." (He was
about 45 years of age.) "The doctors tell me there
is nothing organically wrong with me."

The pain became severe for a moment, and he
grew quiet. I prayed for guidance, having never experienced anything quite like this before.

"Mr. Tam," he continued, "for nine years I've
been searching for God, and if I don't find God
pretty soon, I don't know how I'm going to continue
to exist. I'd about given up, frankly, and then some-

body gave me your book. I can't understand the things you say about your experience, but I believe you're honest."

"We sleep so much better when we are honest," I said, injecting a light note to relieve the intenseness of the moment. Then, bringing the conversation back to its former level, I asked, "Are you a sinner?"

"I'm a very stubborn man," he replied, measuring every word. "If someone had asked me this morning, I'd have said no. But now I've got to say yes."

"Where do sinners go when they die?"

"According to what you've been reading, they go to hell."

"Is that where you want to go?"

"No, of course not."

"How badly do you want to avoid going to hell?"

"What do you mean, Mr. Tam, how bad?"

"Well," I replied, "there's a throne in your life, and I suspect a man by the name of Herschel Jones sits on that throne. Would you be willing to get off that throne and let Jesus Christ sit there as Lord and Savior?"

He thought a moment, then said, "If this is what it takes to have peace in my heart, I'll do it."

We knelt as, tears streaming from his eyes, he confessed to God he was a sinner, that Jesus Christ was the Redeemer, and then he reached out to Him as he prayed, "Lord Jesus, I now receive You as my Lord and Savior."

He later told me that was the hardest sentence he had ever uttered in his life!

He also told me he had driven past our plant

several times, trying to get up enough courage to see me.

So here was an example of "fruit," which, at first glance, seemed to be green—indeed, worm eaten!—but proved to be fully ripe and ready for the plucking.

We use a lot of cardboard for packaging in our plant, and a salesman from a cardboard company called on me regularly for some seven years. He was one of those dapper fellows, a nice enough person to know, but full of all the answers to every subject.

He would deliberately steer our discussions to religion and then tell me what a good churchman he was, how morally he conducted his life, how he read the Bible regularly, believed in Christ.

But it all rang hollow.

I got so I never discussed my faith with him. Instead of "green fruit," I thought here was a case of blemished fruit that would never be fit to pick.

But one day, to my utter amazement, he came into my office and said, "Mr. Tam, you've got something I don't have."

Not even realizing what he was getting at, I asked. "What's that?"

"I have religion," he said, "but you have assurance of eternal life. I don't, but that's sure what I need."

To my amazement, this self-sufficient man was open and ready to receive Christ as his Savior. It had taken a long, long time. So long you might say I actually gave up on him. But surely, though slowly, the seed of the Word of God had taken root in his heart, bringing him to a realization of his need.

In this matter of learning to be perceptive, you need to carefully watch the motivations in people.

I think it was a Moody Bible Institute student who once asked an old fellow in a rescue mission if he was saved.

"Sure, Bud," the man said, "I've been saved at every mission in Chicago!" Then he proceeded on to get his ticket for some free food and a bunk for the night.

I remember the day Bill Haines dropped into the office to ask if I would speak at the Rotary Club in his town about thirty miles south of us.

As we talked, I quietly asked the Holy Spirit to give me perception. I had scarcely breathed the prayer when I became strongly convinced that I must witness to this man.

"Bill," I said, "do you have a problem in your life?"

Growing tensely serious, he said, "I sure do, Mr. Tam."

Closing the door to my office, I asked, "What sort of a problem?"

"I'm an alcoholic and a chain smoker. I've tried to break both of those habits but am powerless."

"Have you tried turning these problems over to God?"

"Yes, I did."

"How was that, Bill?"

"A friend invited me to his church. It was on a Sunday night. The pastor preached such a fantastic sermon that when he gave an invitation for people to come forward, I went. He took me into a side room and prayed with me but nothing happened."

I inquired about the identity of the church, discovered it to be one of the fine evangelical works in his town.

"Bill," I asked, "do you believe in heaven?"

"I sure do."

"Do you believe Jesus Christ is God? That He arose literally from the grave?"

He nodded.

"Do you believe the Bible?"

"Every word of it."

"How about hell?"

He hedged.

"Do you believe in the existence of the devil?"

"No," he admitted sheepishly.

The Holy Spirit had led me to the nub of his problem.

"Why did you go forward in that church meeting, Bill?"

"Because I wanted to lick my bad habits."

"You were looking for reformation. It won't do. What you need is redemption."

I also took him to the sixteenth chapter of Luke.

After I had read the account of the rich man Lazarus, he looked at me in amazement and said, "I didn't know that was in the Bible. If the Bible says there's a hell, then there's a hell, because I believe in the Bible."

I read a verse affirming the existence of Satan.

"If the Bible says there's a devil," he said, "I believe it. Because I believe the Bible."

The Bill Haines story illustrates an enormously

important point. Redd Harper, the beloved composer and cowboy singer, puts it well in his testimony.

"Getting me saved," Redd writes, "wasn't half as difficult as getting me "lost" in the first place. I was so self-righteous, so sure of myself. I'd been a church member for years, gone through all the liturgy. Why, nobody had a right to point to Redd Harper and call him a sinner. But the Bible did. Once I got that through my head, turning to the Savior was a comparatively simple matter."

One of the basic principles in soul winning, then, is that you must get a person lost before you can get him saved.

But you can't do this through mere human ingenuity, however clever you may be. You dare not resort to argument. Be sure your constant prayer is for the Holy Spirit's guidance and empowering.

I believe in being forthright, alert at the task, but I never apply pressure. We are not preachers but witnesses. A witness is a person who shares what has happened to him, what he has seen, what he knows. So when you go out to witness, tell what has happened to you—the joy, the peace, the happiness, the assurance of eternal life blossoming like a garden in your soul.

The Holy Spirit will make your words come alive in the heart of the sinner to whom you witness, awakening in him a desire to have the same experience you have had. You must remember that the whole world is under the burden of guilt, and the whole world is seeking to be free from the burden of guilt. That's why the psychiatrist's calendar is booked weeks in advance.

So when you tell about the peace and fulfillment salvation has brought to your life, the guilt-ridden sinner—however strong his prejudices against the gospel—finds it difficult to argue. But if you pressure, and if you preach, you turn him off and he rejects your witness.

Do be alert for the Holy Spirit's clear guidance to the soul who recognizes his need.

Remember the clear admonition of the scripture, *He that goeth forth and weepeth, bearing precious seed, shall doubtless come again with rejoicing, bringing his sheaves with him.*[4] You may not always get the results you want when you witness. You will be discouraged, when you pour out your heart to a needy soul and he rejects you. That's why you must always remember that the Holy Spirit within you, not you, is the soul winner!

One day a businessman came to my office.

"I'm in bad trouble," he said. "I'm about to go bankrupt. I was talking to a man in my town, and he said you've found an amazing secret to success. I wonder if you'd share it with me?"

"The secret is a very open premise," I said. "I've turned myself, my business, everything I do over to God."

I could see the word disappointment spell out letter after letter across his face.

"I've heard you're strong on religion," he said, "and I've got nothing against that. But it must take more than religion for you to turn the thousands of dollars of profit I understand you make each year."

I asked if I could relate some of my experiences. He agreed. But I suspected he hoped to glean some kınd of fiscal or procedural information from what I said.

I simply told him, as I have told so many times, how I got into the silver reclaiming business, was on the verge of bankruptcy, then felt clearly led of the Holy Spirit to make God my Senior Partner. I told him how my wife and I first turned half of the profits over to Him, then all of the profits.

Then I gave him the simple plan of salvation, asked him if he would open his heart to the Lord Jesus.

He grew cold, restless, soon excused himself and left.

The burden of concern for him remained heavy upon my heart. I felt sure he would return in a day or so, or within the month.

He didn't come back at all.

You see, when I witnessed to him in my office, it was a time of seed planting. The seed had to take root, to grow, before it would be time to pluck the ripe fruit.

A year passed.

Then one day I received a letter from Texas. It was from this businessman. The inevitable had happened. He had gone broke, moved with his family to Texas so he could get away as far as possible from public embarrassment.

But failure stalked him like the plague.

"I couldn't get your testimony out of my mind," he said, "even though at the time I not only rejected what you said, I resented it."

But the seed had been sown, the precious seed of God's eternal, all-powerful Word.

The letter told how he had gone to an evangelical church, had responded to the pastor's invitation to receive Christ as his Savior.

One plants.

Another waters.

God gives the increase!

When we are Master-controlled by the Holy Spirit, it doesn't matter what our particular function happens to be in the work of soul winning.

But we must be Master-controlled!

And no two people alike, no two situations.

No pat procedures in witnessing.

But one element remains constant—the sure guidance, the unlimited power and wisdom, of the Holy Spirit deep within us.

Yes, to some we plant seed. To others we water the good ground. And then sometimes we have the joy of the harvest. But the important thing . . . always . . . is to recognize that it is the Holy Spirit who does the work through us, often in spite of us, if we will only let him do his work.

Know ye not that ye are the temple of God—lay a firm hold on that fact, friend—*and that the Spirit of God dwelleth in you?* [5]

[1] Hebrews 4:12.
[2] Revelation 20:12, 13, 15.
[3] Hebrews 4:12.
[4] Psalm 126:6.
[5] I Corinthians 3:16.

CHAPTER TEN
HOARD YOUR FAITH, OR INVEST IT

In the early days of my Christian life, I came to a western city, booked a hotel room, went up the elevator without bothering to first take some food.

Because business had been miserable.

Discouraged, homesick, feeling sorry for myself, I threw myself halfway upon the bed, slid to my knees.

The way too many of us Christians do when we pray, I fell error to a bad case of the "gimmies." Half-whimpering, I reminded God I was His child—as though He didn't already know!—and that He had promised to supply all my needs. If the promises in the Bible were so wonderful, as I had heard preachers eloquently declare them to be, why had I gone to photographer's studio after photographer's studio without placing more than a handful of our Tamco silver collectors?

"You've got to give me some business, God," I implored. "I'm running out of money. I might not even have enough to get back home."

Then God did something to me He had never done before as a distinct answer to my prayers.

He rebuked me.

Clearly, in the more than audible listening chambers of the heart, I heard my Lord say, "Why should I help you? What do you do for me?"

"I do a lot of things, Lord." I responded, feeling the rebuke but hopeful of getting somewhere in my intercession. "I go to church every Sunday, to every midweek service. Even when I'm on the road like this, I always look up a church I can attend."

"Of course, Stanley, I see you in church. But you know why you go. You want to find some new promise from the Bible that will benefit you materially. What do you do for me?"

"I pray twice a day."

"You should have a recording of your prayers, Stanley. It's gimmie, gimmie, gimmie. What do you do for me?"

"I read the Bible every morning and every night."

"But it's the same as when you go to church, isn't it—looking for promises to benefit yourself? What do you do for me?"

Like a falchion in the dark, the question cut me to the conscience, haunted me into the night.

"What do you do for me?"

I searched my heart, searched it as I had never done before, opening doors long closed to the secret of my innermost desires and motivations. I saw myself living a self-centered Christian life, worshipping

God, reading my Bible, praying, but always with one prime motivation—to see what I could get out of Christianity for number one.

That night the Holy Spirit emblazoned another word upon my mind, my conscience.

Others!

Still too timid at that point to launch out onto overt witnessing, I began giving out tracts. Evenings, when I over-nighted away from home, I went out onto the street corners. I did this in some thirty states.

You see, the problem with too many Christians is that they are spiritual misers. They may have great knowledge of the Bible. It thrills them to read the tremendous promises God gives in His Word. They know exactly what verses to lay hold upon in times of adversity.

But they store up these eternal treasures in the counting houses of their own selfish little castles. While multitudes pass their gates, hungering for the bread of life, they give no heed, show no concern.

They are stingy.

I remember that word stingy from childhood—friends who would not share candy, toys, who always wanted to keep everything for themselves. No stinginess can compare, however, with that of a Christian who possesses in his mind the knowledge of the gospel and keeps it to himself instead of investing it in the lives of others!

There is a statement in Scripture which I know applies primarily to materialism.

But it has overtones here.

Do not store up for yourselves treasures on earth, where moth and rust destroy and where thieves break in and steal. But store up for yourselves treasures in heaven, where moth and rust do not destroy, and where thieves do not break in and steal. For where your treasure is, there your heart will be also.[1]

Where do you keep your treasure?

You know, Satan doesn't mind it too much if you are what we normally classify as a good Christian. Attend church regularly. Contribute substantially to the church budget. Be willing to serve on committees, in church offices, even as a Sunday school teacher. All good in themselves.

But Satan doesn't want you to get involved in rescuing the perishing!

Do you know how Satan does this? He can't get inside you, because the Holy Spirit lives there. But he has other tactics so subversive you won't know he is at work unless you keep constantly alert. That's why the Bible cautions, *Do not grieve the Holy Spirit.*[2]

I'm afraid Satan succeeds in causing the vast majority of God's children to grieve the Holy Spirit, however, thus preventing the Holy Spirit from flowing out creatively in touching the lives of others with the power of the gospel.

Here's how Satan does it.

Love not the world, the Bible cautions, *neither the things that are in the world. If any man love the world, the love of the Father is not in him.*

See how aptly that warning relates to the earlier quotation concerning the laying up of treasures.

For all that is in the world, the Bible continues *the lust of the flesh, and the lust of the eyes, and the pride of life, is not of the Father, but is of the world, and the world passeth away, and the lust of it; But he that doeth the will of God abideth forever.*[3]

Now lets note some very important truths in that passage of scripture.

The foremost objective, as pointed out in the quotation, is the doing of *the will of God.*

What is the will of God?

First and foremost—may you never forget it—is for His children to serve as instruments through whom the Holy Spirit can convey God's love to others.

What is it then that keeps a Christian from discovering this *will of God?*

Look earlier in the quotation.

First of all, we are warned to *love not the world.*

And how is the world characterized?

The lust of the flesh.

The lust of the eyes.

The pride of life.

Those are the three areas whereby Satan attacks the Christian, grieving the Holy Spirit, keeping the Christian from living out the will of God in his life.

If you hoard your faith, in all likelihood it is either because you allow *the lust of the flesh* or *the lust of the eyes* or *the pride of life,* or all three, to keep you from being obedient to your Lord's directives.

Now let me underscore this with a very important point of information. The epistles of John, from which the above quotation is taken, were written to believers, not to unbelievers. So, you see, the warning is to the faithful rather than to the wayward.

In fact, do you know that most of the areas in the Bible, where we are warned against the tactics of the devil, are addressed directly to Christians?

Satan doesn't need to exert much craft against the man steeped in sin. He already has him. But Satan practices his most clever wiles against the Christian, determined to keep the Christian from fulfilling God's plan for his life.

A shoe sure to pinch a lot of feet is the one that says the reason so many Christians give little thought to the devil is because they're doing exactly what he wants them to do—going through the motions of a sincere Christian experience while they resist the Holy Spirit's sovreign claim upon their lives.

Still another area of the Bible relates with devastating implications to this matter of spiritual hoarding.

I think multitudes of twentieth century evangelicals might have felt quite at home as members of the New Testament church at Corinth. Because anyone who likes to have one foot in the world and one foot in the church, who wants all the blessings of heaven and all the joys of earth, would have been completely at ease on the back pew in the Corinth sanctuary. The Apostle Paul told those Corinthians he *could not speak unto you as unto spiritual, but as unto carnal, even as unto babes in Christ. I have fed you with milk, and not with solid food.*[4]

Yet, although this was the weak church of the New Testament—perhaps *because* it was the weak church of the New Testament—Paul unfolded in his letters to Corinth some of the greatest basic truths we can know as Christians.

He spoke succinctly of life investment, when he told the Corinthians, *other foundation can no man lay than that which is laid, which is Jesus Christ. Now if any man build upon this foundation gold, silver, precious stones, wood, hay, stubble—every man's work shall be made manifest; for the day shall declare it, because it shall be revealed by fire; and the fire shall test every man's work of what sort it is. If any man's work abide which he hath built upon it, he shall receive a reward. If any man's work shall be burned, he shall suffer loss; but he himself shall be saved, yet as by fire.*[5]

Please take a moment to read those words again.

They are eternally important—to you!

Don't proceed to my next paragraph until you do. And, as you read, invite the Holy Spirit to show you the staggering truth to which these verses relate in the matter of your eternal investments.

Now, for a moment, imagine yourself as a miser.

Through the years of a long life, you have lived frugally, hoarding to yourself every possible penny.

Let's say you have a particular penchant for fifty dollar bills. You have kept a container for coins, counting them often. Whenever the coins totaled fifty dollars, you've taken them to the bank and exchanged them for one of the coveted bills. You've done the same with your larger earnings, reducing everything to the fifty dollar note.

You have boxes of these fifty dollar bills hidden in some remote cranny of your house.

Then one day, as you count the coins and discover

you have just over fifty dollars worth, you again trudge to the bank.

But, returning to within sight of your home, panic strikes you heart.

Your house is in flames!

You run to it, try to enter, can't. Your own life is spared but all those fifty dollar bills go up in smoke, uninsured.

That illustrates what the Bible is talking about here.

Gold, silver, precious stones represent the work of the Holy Spirit, enriching our lives. *Wood, hay, stubble* speak of those transient investments, that selfish hoarding, which can never withstand the fire of God's judgement.

This all suggests to me a vitally important function, which ought to be at the top of the agenda of every Christians life.

Remembering back to chapter one, when we examined the basic premise of this book—soul winners who don't win souls—we understand that it is the right and privilege of every Christian to share in the supreme act of creation, namely bringing new life through the new birth to those who do not know Christ.

How exciting it must have been for our Lord to place Andromeda some two and one half billion light years out into space. Who knows what lies beyond that magnificent galaxy? What a joy it must have been to turn the earth green with trees and grass, make it fragrant with flowers.

And what a glorious moment when the Trinity declared in unison those creative words, *let us make man in our image, after our likeness.*[6]

But no act of creation, primordial or present, can equal that of being privileged to touch a life, *dead in sins,*[7] and see it born anew. *If any man be in Christ,* the Bible tells us, describing conversion, *he is a new creation.*[8]

It is impossible for one to invest time and talent more effectively!

The Christian must be constantly alert, sensitive to any moment when the Holy Spirit may be grieved through our selfish attention to *the things of this world.* Surely this is what Paul talked about when he wrote, *I am crucified with Christ; nevertheless I live; yet not I, but Christ liveth in me; and the life I now live in the flesh I live by the faith of the Son of God, who loved me and gave Himself for me.*[9]

We don't become morbid about such things, grovelling in despair for fear of doing something, thinking a casual thought, which might grieve the Holy Spirit. Quite to the contrary, this can be the most positive experience a Christian can know—opening one's self totally to the creative flow of the Holy Spirit.

Let the Holy Spirit control your thoughts. Invite His guidance when you read the scriptures. Expect the Holy Spirit to lead you, as you meet people.

God intends your life to be endowed with joy. But with that joy comes responsibility. Only a fool wants to live in perpetual frivolity. Though we do experience joy, we also share the Savior's concern.

135

EVERY CHRISTIAN A SOUL WINNER

And how enriching even that can be!

It all totals the sure, sustaining guidance of the Holy Spirit in response to our obedience.

Again and again in my life, this involves sheer adventure.

For example, I received a telephone call one day from a pastor in Niagara Falls, Ontario, inviting me to speak at his missionary convention. He wanted me for a Friday night, told me he would arrange Saturday and Sunday appointments.

All went well until Sunday afternoon.

As is my custom, I went to my room that afternoon to meditate on the scriptures and pray for God's special guidance on the meeting. But for some strange reason, my prayers seemed to hit the ceiling and bounce right back to me.

Finally, in desperation, I asked, "Lord, what's wrong?"

Like a lightning bolt, a name flashed across my mind.

Dr. Collins.

The thought of that man tortured my conscience.

A year previous, I had been in Chicago on a business trip, spending a week at a hotel.

The first day, I was able to park my car near a recreation area. That evening, making my way toward the car, a girls' softball team caught my attention. They were quite good and I became so interested in watching them I began walking sideways and, because of this, ran into a concrete lamp post.

The collision broke my glasses and cut a gash in my eyebrow.

I hurried to my hotel, where the hotel physician

took nine stitches in my wound, instructed me to return to his office on Wednesday so he could check for possible infection.

I came as he instructed.

He wasn't busy that afternoon, and we began chatting. Twice in the conversation he made statements which gave me a perfect opportunity to witness.

But I selfishly hoarded my faith!

From the moment I left his office, conviction nagged at me like a sickness. The conviction continued until I could only assuage it by purchasing a book, containing the witness of a Christian doctor, which I mailed to the hotel physician, Dr. Collins.

So there I was at Niagara Falls, Ontario, a year later, asking God to make me a blessing to people in the Sunday evening service.

"Why should I help you in the service tonight," the Lord seemed to chide, "when you failed so miserably back there in Chicago? The pastor here called and made an appointment for you to speak in this church. The Holy Spirit made an appointment for you to witness to Dr. Collins. But you didn't do it."

"That was a year ago, Lord," I argued. "And Chicago is a long ways away. You know how repentent I've been. I did send the doctor a book."

But I couldn't get any peace in my heart, until I said, "Lord, I promise that, with your help, I'll call this doctor as soon as I get home and make an appointment to see him."

Immediately, the presence of the Lord filled that room and peace came to my heart.

There were nearly four hundred people in attendance at the evening service. Frankly, my host had fed me so well I found it difficult to speak. Yet, in a wonderful way, the Holy Spirit loosened my tongue and enabled me to give fluent testimony.

When I extended the invitation, three came forward. Then a gentleman slipped out of his seat. (I later learned he was the Sunday school superintendent.) After him came three more.

Then a lady.

And then, as though an electric shock struck the entire church, people began coming from all directions.

During the singing of the invitation hymn, the pastor suddenly stopped in the middle of a stanza, put down his hymnal, and went to the altar himself to stand beside one of the women.

His wife.

They had an inquiry room, but it was too small for such a large group.

I said, "Pastor, what shall we do?"

"Mr. Tam," he managed to reply, "I'm so under conviction myself, have such great spiritual need, you just go ahead and do as the Holy Spirit leads you."

I began to offer an audible prayer for the group, then discovered no one was listening.

So great was the feeling of conviction.

"Does someone have something you'd like to say?" I asked.

Immediately, a lady spoke up to say, "I've been taking money out of the cash register where I work.

Tomorrow I'm going to my boss and confess and make restitution."

Another man said, "I've been delivering milk in the city for four years but have never witnessed to one of my customers. I'm starting this week."

"I've attended school here for three years," a young lady said, "and have never told one of my classmates that I'm a Christian."

Then the pastor's wife turned and, with much difficulty, said, "I have a confession to make to this congregation. I've been teaching the soul winners' class for five years now. But I have to confess to you that I've never won one soul to Jesus Christ since I became a Christian!"

The meeting lasted until ten o'clock.

You see, there was nothing so unique or powerful in my testimony. But I had obeyed the voice of the Holy Spirit when He spoke to me concerning the doctor in Chicago.

And obedience opens the door for the Holy Spirit to flow out in blessing to others through our lives.

When I got back to my home in Lima, Ohio, I called Doctor Collins in Chicago. He gave me an appointment for three o'clock on Friday afternoon.

Unfortunately, whereas he had not been busy when my first opportunity came, this Friday was a busy day, with his office full of patients. Finally, the nurse called me, took me to one of the examination rooms.

My mind went blank.

What would I say?

Would this learned man think me a fool for travelling over two hundred miles to talk to him about religion?

How wonderful it is in times like this to simply put oneself into the hands of the Holy Spirit!

Moments later, the door opened. Doctor Collins, my file card in his hand, appeared.

"How is your eye, Mr. Tam?" he asked pleasantly.

"My eye is fine," I said.

He grew momentarily perplexed.

"I suppose I'm the strangest patient you've ever had," I continued.

"Why?" he asked.

"Because I've come all the way to Chicago to talk to you about your soul."

"Oh, yes," he said quietly, without so much as a hint of hostility touching his attitude, "I remember you. You sent me the book about the doctor. I read it. I'm interested. Do you have anything else I could read?"

"Could I give you my personal testimony?" I asked.

He nodded.

As quickly as I could, I told him what God had done. Then I talked to him about his own need.

For fifteen minutes he did not so much as glance at his watch. Then he said, "Mr. Tam, as you saw, I have an office full of patients. I can't give you any more time. But let me express my deepest appreciation to you for having come to Chicago to talk to me about my soul."

I didn't have the privilege of leading Doctor Collins to a definite decision that day. But I do know I obeyed the prompting of the Holy Spirit in calling him and making the appointment.

Obedience.

This is the beating heart of successful witness.

Obedience and daily spiritual cleansing.

Both the office work of the Holy Spirit in our lives!

[1] Matthew 6:19-21.
[2] Ephesians 4:30.
[3] I John 2:15-17.
[4] I Corinthians 3:12.
[5] I Corinthians 3:11-15.
[6] Genesis 1:26.
[7] Ephesians 2:5.
[8] II Corinthians 5:17.
[9] Galatians 2:20.

CHAPTER ELEVEN
STILL SHY? TRY TEAMWORK!

Holding soul winning clinics all across North America as I do, I meet all kinds of people, hear all kinds of reasons why Christians find it difficult to witness.

"I just don't have the courage," I'm often told. "I'm so shy."

Because shyness underlined so much of my earlier life, particularly my first efforts at witnessing, I try to be understanding. Yet I also remember how wonderfully the Holy Spirit led me out of shyness into the boldness that comes from obedience.

I realize I may have had latent capacities sublimated by a veneer of shyness. As I sought the inner cleansing of the Holy Spirit, as by faith I put my life into His control, it may well be these latent abilities surfaced, becoming gifts of the Holy Spirit in an unique sense. I also realize others may have personality deficits, humanly speaking, which make it extremely difficult for them to share their faith.

As I say, I try to be understanding to such people.

If lack of courage, or outright shyness, hinder you in your desire to witness, try teamwork. Ask some Christian, already successful as a soul winner, if you can work together with him.

When Jesus sent out His diciples on those first witnessing assignments, His plan was *to send them forth by two and two.*[1]

God told Moses that one might chase a thousand but two could *put ten thousand to flight.*[2]

I have met people who found it extremely difficult to witness by themselves but shared their faith effectively when working with someone else. Most church visitation programs involve the two together procedure.

I must add a couple of painful paragraphs at this point, however.

I stand firmly in favor of the evangelical church, reluctant to criticize it outwardly or by innuendo, but I fear visitation programs—in which the objective is to invite people to attend your church, send their children to your Sunday school—may be a means of salving the consciences of some Christians who ought to be actively witnessing.

Of course, people can find Christ in the church sanctuary. Though I am a layman, with no theological or homiletical training, it has been my privilege many times to speak in churches when, at the giving of a public invitation, people have come to the altar seeking salvation. The Bible is very clear about the need for a public confession of faith—*if thou shalt confess with thy mouth the Lord Jesus*—[3] and for a sinner to make his way to the altar can be a very visible way of letting people know he desires to make a complete U-turn in the direction of his life.

But in my own experience, I have found it much more natural to lead people to Christ in surroundings familiar to them, rather than imposing a church scene upon them in which to be converted. Once they have trusted Christ, I urge them to make this known by their own word of mouth witness. I also strongly emphasize that they immediately begin attending and, as soon as they qualify, join a good evangelical church.

I have noted, too, the growing number of pastors who, when they give an invitation, invite those seeking help to come to the pastor's study or to call the pastor for an appointment at his home or office. I'm sure the reason the inquiry or counselling room procedure developed over the years in many groups, instead of doing personal work at the church altar, was so the seeker could be put more at ease and counselling accomplished more effectively.

But whatever the pastor's procedure may be, I do want to strongly indicate the effectiveness in many churches of teamwork which involves the layman and his pastor. Out in the marketplace, where the layman has rapport, he makes contact with needy hearts. When he finds a seeker, but does not feel he can personally bring the seeker to a knowledge of salvation, he suggests they call on the pastor.

So, if you are still shy at witnessing, do try this principle of teamwork. Unless the Holy Spirit very definitely leads you to do so, however, do not think of this as the ultimate in your witnessing. Think of it as a time of apprenticeship, as you gain courage and learn good procedure from watching others.

You see, the time could well come when you will find yourself in a situation where the factors involved will not permit bringing in your pastor or another layman. It will be completely a solo flight for you. When that time comes, you will want to be able to complete the transaction yourself.

If the thought of such a circumstance makes you nervous, let me again emphasize that it is the Holy Spirit within you, not you, who is the soul winner. Be continually alert for His leading. Keep your thoughts and motives clean. See yourself continually as having been designed by the Creator for the prime purpose of sharing His grace with others.

Something very wonderful could happen.

You might begin as an apprentice, depending upon your pastor or another layman for support in witnessing. Then, as you mature spiritually, you will launch out by yourself. And then—it can surely happen!—the time could well come when you will provide support for someone else new in the gathering of harvest.

The healthy Christian experience is one which you *grow in grace, and in the knowledge of the Lord and Savior, Jesus Christ.*[4]

That verse is not only an admonition but your divine right as a child of God!

In my own experience, as the Lord used me more and more in witnessing, I began to have the opportunity of helping others less experienced. I have no desire whatever for fame. But it does please me, and I try always to give glory to God, when I realize that people think of Stanley Tam as a soul winner. I just don't know a higher honor than that.

When you do mature to this wonderful privilege of serving as a team captain, you will need to be especially on guard. The junior member of your association may be one of those well-meaning Christians who are long on zeal and short of wisdom. Or it may simply be a matter of the unique nature of a situation.

I received a phone call one day from a friend of mine who asked if I would come down to the print shop as he had something he needed to discuss.

I went immediately.

He told me he had been talking to a young man whom he believed to be ready to accept Christ.

"You know how it is with me," my friend said. "I want to reach people for Christ, but I just don't quite seem to have the knack for closing the deal. So I talked to him about you. He said he'd be willing to talk to you. He's an artist, a sign painter, and I get the impression he and his wife are having marriage problems. He's waiting at his house but I don't think that that's the best place to talk to him."

We took the young fellow to my office.

Since he had had a Sunday school background, we began with John 3:16. Then we showed him that *all have sinned, and come short of the glory of God.*[5] We had him read those words from Isaiah, *all we like sheep have gone astray; we have turned every one to his own way, and the Lord hath laid on him the iniquity of us all.*[6] Then we took him to the Gospel of John and had him read, *as many as received him, to them gave he power to become the children of God, even to them that believe on his name.*[7]

As we knelt, the young man prayed, acknowledging his sin, his need of salvation, and asked the Lord Jesus to come into his heart.

Since he had no church home, we invited him to our church the following Sunday.

But he didn't come.

We called on him Monday, invited him to our Bible study and prayer meeting.

He said he would come.

But didn't.

Nor did he attend services the following Sunday.

After contacting him several times in the next few months, it became obvious he had not really accepted Christ, as there was no evidence of change in his life, no desire for fellowship with Christians.

"What shall we do?" my friend asked. "Do you think I pushed him too soon?"

"There's no point in trying to pick fruit until it's ripe," I told him.

"Do we give up?"

"Not at all. We stop going to see him. But let's pray for him more than ever."

Let me insert something here.

When you endeavor to lead someone to Christ but seemingly fail, it may often be wise to stop calling on the person. Be sure you have carefully planted the seed of God's Word and, if possible, nurtured it with your own testimony, with careful counsel, with a loving and helpful spirit.

Then leave the person alone for awhile.

During this time, you not only pray for the person, you pray for yourself. True, the Lord may lead this one to another Christian, who will have the joy of reaping. That option should be part of your prayer. But you should also pray that the Holy Spirit may give you sure guidance to know when you should perhaps once again demonstrate initiative on behalf of the one you wish to reach.

In my case with the young sign painter, a year passed and the time came for a large photographers' convention. We needed a new display sign. Immediately, the Holy Spirit brought this man's name to my mind.

I called him, asked him if he could do the job for us.

He was busy during the day but offered to come to the plant in the evening. I immediately agreed to this, sensing the hand of the Holy Spirit creating the best possible climate for successful witness!

Of course, the very first evening I wanted to re-open spiritual negotiations.

No opportunity presented itself.

I prayed and prayed.

But the Holy Spirit restrained.

The project was sizeable, so he came several evenings. My friend the printer and I kept up lively telephone conversations during the day.

"I've got people all over town praying for that guy!" the printer said.

When the final night for the project came, the young man arrived with a black eye and a cut lip. I didn't press him for particulars but sensed an intense urging of the Holy Spirit to consummate my witness.

Yet, throughout the evening, no opportunity presented itself.

So, when he finished, I said, "Like to go out and get a milkshake? You've been working hard enough to build up a good appetite. There's a hamburger shop down the road."

He was very agreeable.

As we sat at the table drinking, the conversation opened beautifully, making it completely natural for me to say, "Satan doesn't have much to offer does he? Only pain, difficulty and heartache."

I once again presented the plan of salvation, concluding with John 1:12.

"To as many as received him, Floyd, "I said, "That includes you and me. *To them gave He power to become the children of God."*

I could see the Holy Spirit intervening, complete change coming to the young man's attitude.

I wanted to press for a decision there in the hamburger shop but felt definitely led to wait till we got to the car.

Then I said, "Floyd, the Lord is speaking to you tonight, and I know you're listening. He wants you to accept Him now. I don't understand what happened when you came to my office, but I know Christ did not become your Savior, because your life hasn't changed. But tonight you can make a decision and become a new man."

"You mean right here in your car?" he asked.

I might have answered glibly, "You can take Christ into your life any place, Floyd," but the Holy Spirit alerted me to a possible implication in the tone of his voice.

Breathing a prayer for guidance, I said, "I have the keys to our church in my pocket. We can go there by ourselves, kneel at the altar if you wish, and you can accept Christ as your Savior. Or we could go to my office. Or, frankly, you could open your heart to Christ right here in the car."

He hesitated a moment, said, "Let's go to the church."

We had a midnight evangelistic service in our church that night, with just the illumination of a couple of lights at the back of the sanctuary.

As we knelt at the altar, I prayed for Floyd, then took time to once more spell out the promises God gives to seeking sinners.

Spontaneously, Floyd poured out his heart to the Lord, and this time I knew he understood the plan of salvation and meant it.

Today this young man is an active church member, head of a Christian family, living victoriously.

Many times I thank God for letting me be on the team that brought him through to victory!

Evangelistic campaigns provide an excellent opportunity for teamwork. Many evangelists use the "Operation Andrew" approach, encouraging Christians to bring their friends to the meetings.

It was my privilege one year to serve as chairman of the citywide evangelistic crusade in our community.

At the close of the campaign, I got a phone call

from an elderly lady who had seen me on the platform night after night and heard me give my testimony.

"Would you please come and talk to my husband?" she said. "He wasn't well enough to get out to the meetings."

Calling at the home, I found that the wife had done a good job of planting and watering the seed. It was a simple matter for me to bring this man to a salvation decision.

The woman told me about her son, who also lived in our town. She had prayed for him for many years, longing to see him come to Christ. He and his wife were having a lot of trouble, she said, and asked me to talk to them.

I did.

The couple received me cordially but did not openly respond to the gospel.

A year after the conversion of her husband, however, I received another phone call from the lady.

"I've got to talk to you," she said.

She caught me on a very busy week and I began making excuses.

"It's very urgent," she said. "I have to see you as soon as possible."

So I arranged to meet with her.

She told me her son's marriage was on the rocks, so I agreed to go see him the next afternoon.

When I arrived at the house, he was coming out the door. He told me he and his wife had talked things over, were planning a divorce. From the anguish on his face, it was plain to see he didn't like this kind of solution to their problems.

We slipped back into the house.

It was a different setting now. He did not put up any resistance or avoid the gospel. After a few moments together, he willingly knelt and asked the Lord Jesus into his heart.

Piecing the story together, I discovered that—when he saw his marriage going to pieces—he planned suicide. Two members of the family, coming to the house, found him in a drunken slumber, with two loaded guns and a suicide note.

But now his life became transformed. He went to his wife, told her what had happened, and I subsequently received a telephone call from her saying she wanted to talk with me.

So I returned to their home, had the joy of seeing the young woman trust the Savior and then watch, unable to keep tears from my eyes, as the two put their arms around each other and dedicated their lives and their family to Christ.

It wouldn't have happened, however, without teamwork!

Another time a young man in our church came to me and said, "The foreman down where I work is sick. Would you go talk to him? I'm afraid he wouldn't listen to me."

He told me the man was about fifty years old, had never gone to church in his life. He had a vile temper, a life pock-marked with bad habits.

"He acts like he's a nervous wreck half the time," the young man said.

I decided this fellow was a little too rough for me to handle so didn't go see him.

At church the following Sunday morning, the

young man asked, "Did you go see my boss this week?"

I gave a lame excuse.

The third week came.

Another attempted excuse. But I could see how disappointed my young friend was.

So I said, "I'll go see him tomorrow night, I promise."

"Please don't tell him I sent you." the man said.

"Well," I hedged, "I'll need some kind of introduction. I just can't walk in on him."

"But if you use my name, and it backfires, I'll lose my job."

I gave the appointment much prayer concern, decided on a plan. Obtaining some of our church literature, I canvassed the block where the man lived. Thus, when I came to his house, I truthfully said, "I've been calling on homes in the area, inviting people who don't attend elsewhere to come to our church. Do you by chance have a church you regularly attend?"

He shook his head.

Then, to my encouragement, he asked, "Where is your church?"

I told him.

"I couldn't go that far," he said. "I don't have a car. It's too far away."

He mentioned a church nearby to which some of his neighbors had invited him. It was one of the fine evangelical churches in our town.

"That's a very good church," I said. "After all,

you know, it isn't the church we attend that gets us to heaven."

"What do you mean the church doesn't get you to heaven?" he asked dubiously. "How else you gonna get there?"

"Would you like me to tell you how to get to heaven?" I asked.

"Well," he replied, "if the church doesn't get you to heaven, I'd sure like to know how you get there."

"I have a film on the plan of salvation," I said. "It tells you how to get to heaven. Could I show it to you?"

He was agreeable.

So I brought in my projector and set it up in his living room. I watched him closely as the film played upon the screen. He sat tense, taking in every word.

Yet, when the film was over, I felt no liberty to press him for a decision.

You see, in this teamwork business, we don't just work with other people. We work with the Holy Spirit. And the Holy Spirit gave me no clear guidance to try to bring this man to a decision.

He followed me to the car, as I took out the projector. Plainly, he was interested.

"Would you like me to come back in a couple weeks and talk to you more about this?" I asked.

"I sure would," he said.

I couldn't wait for two weeks.

After a week went by, I called him.

"I've got another film you might like to see," I said.

He invited me back.

This time his wife and his grandfather were there. Immediately after the film finished, everybody got up and left the room except the man and myself. It was just as if it were planned.

"Mr. Gillroy," I said, "I've been watching you, praying for you during the film. I believe tonight is the night you should receive Jesus Christ as your Savior. Would there be anything to keep you from doing it?"

He looked at the floor for a long time, then said, "No, I don't guess there would be."

"I understand you've never gone to church," I said.

"That's correct," he said.

"Have you ever prayed?"

"Never in all my life."

"Well," I said, "it isn't what you pray that really matters, it's what you do with your heart and your life. If you'll just turn your life completely to the Lord, he'll come in and save you."

We slipped over to the couch and knelt.

He mumbled a few inaudible words.

Just a bit confused, I put my hand on his shoulder, and was about to speak a word of encouragement.

Then he turned to me, tears streaming down his cheeks.

"It's gone!" he gasped.

"What's gone, Bill?" I asked.

"A load I've been carrying on my chest for years!"

In that miraculous, transforming moment, the power of the gospel had turned Bill Gillroy from a sinner to a saint!

But that was only the beginning of the story.

The following Thursday I dropped by to see how he was doing. His daughter met me at the door.

"Dad's not here," she said. "He couldn't wait till Sunday, so he took Mother and they went to the little church down the street."

My heart sang praise to God!

"We've got a new Dad," the daughter continued. "He used to have a vile temper, always took it out on Mom and us kids. But this week it only got away from him twice. Each time he actually apologized to us."

Bill Gillroy did become a new creation through his faith in Jesus Christ. His neighbors, the men down at the shop, everyone who knew him was amazed at the miracle.

God gave him deliverance, too, from the habits which had enslaved him for so many years.

But Bill Gillroy not only came to Christ as the result of teamwork and soul winning, he wanted to get on the team himself. One day he called me and said, "Stanley, I want to be a soulwinner like you. Could I go on some of your house calls?"

I was delighted to have him, saw him grow in maturity, learn quickly the tactics of good witnessing.

Then at two o'clock one morning, his phone rang. It was his daughter.

"Dad," she said, "my husband and I can't sleep. We are under such conviction. If we come over right now, will you pray with us?"

"Come right on over!" Bill exhuded.

When he hung up the phone, however, he realized he wasn't all that sure of himself in witnessing. So, as a good junior team member, he called the pastor. When the young couple arrived, the pastor was there.

"We didn't sleep all night," Bill told me. "It took no time at all for them to get things settled with the Lord. Then we spent the rest of the time till morning just praising the Lord together!"

Down the street a couple of blocks from Bill's house was a man dying of silicosis, caused by working in one of the steel foundaries in our city.

Bill and I called on him again and again.

He listened, sometimes asked questions, but kept his heart hardened to the gospel appeal.

One day I said, "Bill, I'm not going back to see him anymore."

"Do you mind if I take over," Bill asked.

For two years, every Sunday, Bill took Sunday school papers to the man. Before the man died, he said to Bill, "I knew you before you became a Christian. I've watched you since. There's a tremendous difference. I'm ready to accept Jesus Christ."

Still unsure of himself, Bill again played the roll of a junior team member and called his pastor.

But it wasn't long until Bill was on his own. In fact, he became the captain of a soul winning team, joined by one of the young men from our church.

At the end of the first year of their teamwork together, I asked, "Bill, how many souls did the Lord give you this past year?"

"We've seen thirty three decisions." Bill said.

Teamwork!

Laborers together with God! [8]

STILL SHY? TRY TEAMWORK!

[1] Mark 6:7.
[2] Deuteronomy 32:30.
[3] Romans 10:9.
[4] II Peter 3:18.
[5] Romans 3:23.
[6] Isaiah 53:6.
[7] John 1:12.
[8] I Corinthians 3:9.

CHAPTER TWELVE
ZERO IN ON WIDE HORIZONS

Soul winning is big business.

The biggest business in the world.

People who go out witnessing in a shabby way, who carry on like fanatics, discredit the very name of Jesus Christ.

I can't over-emphasize the fact that, when we witness, we represent the Creator of the universe. And His supreme act did not consist of creating that universe but in designing the plan of salvation.

And speaking of big business, I meet people who like to drop names. They claim to have met men in Washington politics, in New York finance. But no human encounter can provide even shadow comparison to the high echelon relationship you will enjoy with the Holy Spirit. Now, as you think of such potential encounter, the prospect may seem nebulous.

Let me assure you of some very real truths.

The Holy Spirit is a person. People who speak of

the Holy Spirit as "it" are rude, whether intentionally or unintentionally. As a person, the Holy Spirit can become very personal in your experience.

"The Holy Spirit," Jesus said, *"whom the Father will send in my name, he shall teach you all things."* [1]

You can't enter into a profound student/teacher relationship with an "it"!

And as you mature in your spiritual life, you will perceive deeper and deeper truths related to the Holy Spirit and will experience increasingly more intimate and profound dimensions of this intensely personal relationship.

Intimacy with the Holy Spirit doesn't make you some kind of far out kook. Intimacy with the Holy Spirit makes you a warmly genuine human being who can relate to other human beings.

You want His specific direction. You want to know that the people to whom you witness are those to whom you have been led by the Holy Spirit. You need to be confident that, when you speak with one to whom you have been led, your words spring forth from the very wisdom of the Holy Spirit within you.

The one-to-one relationship of soul winner to seeker will become increasingly meaningful to you.

Never lose sight of that one-to-one quotient.

I have no opposition to mass evangelism properly conducted. The important thing is for people to come to Christ. I do know, if only from my own experience, how easy it is to develop a complex by which you want to bring in an evangelist to do the work you should be doing, to hire a preacher to win the souls you should win.

I can only come back again and again to what the Bible says.

To what the Lord Jesus said.

"I am the vine," He tells us, *"ye are the branches. He that abideth in me, and I in him, the same bringeth forth much fruit."* [2]

I want to be a fruit bearing Christian, don't you?

I don't simply want to be content to sit in the bleachers and watch someone else play the game. I want to be part of the conflict with evil, to share the sweet taste of victory when a soul is snatched out of the very fire of hell through the redeeming power of the gospel.

By the way, has anyone ever shared with you the mathematics of one-to-one witnessing?

Suppose you were the only Christian in the world —no one else, just you. What should you do?

Find yourself a haven to hide away from the evil world?

No, in one year's time you could win one person to Jesus Christ. So then at the end of the first year, there would be two Christians in the world.

What would you do? Find a haven where you two lonely saints could fellowship together awaiting your release from this evil world?

No, each of you could win a soul during the second year.

At the conclusion of that year, then, there would be four Christians in the world.

At the end of the third year eight.

The fourth year, sixteen.

And on and on.

Do you know how long, with each Christian winning just one soul to Christ every twelve months, it would take to reach the whole world?

Only thirty three years!

It thrilled me, as I became more and more experienced in witnessing, to see people come one by one to a knowledge of my Savior. But though many came, and I praise God for each of them, I couldn't rest on past laurels. What of the multitudes more whom I might be able to touch, if I could only get to them?

My horizons began to widen.

We started putting gospel tracts into every package shipped out from our business. We continue to do this.

Through these tracts, many have come to know Christ. Some have contacted us, and I have been able to follow through personally. Or refer them to someone nearby who could help them.

The publication of my story in the book GOD OWNS MY BUSINESS, and the subsequent release of the motion picture under the same title, opened more doors for us. Every month, without fail, people come to the Savior because of these widened horizons of witness.

A businessman called me from the West Coast, said he had to see me right away on an important matter. I was extremely busy at the time, getting out our new catalog, and tried to put him off. But he insisted he had to come.

So he flew all the way to Lima to spend a couple of hours in my office.

"I read your book," he said, "and I've got to have what you've got."

It was my joy to lead him to Christ!

The pastor of a large liberal church in the Greater Los Angeles area read the book, opened his heart to the Savior.

"I was considering dropping out of the ministry," he said in an article published by the Los Angeles Times. "Previous to accepting Christ, my life was in turmoil, my church was declining, and I was discouraged.

"But since my conversion, God has moved powerfully in my life and in my church, with many others turning their lives over to Christ and really experiencing the power of love. We have watched life after life really change as they have received Christ. A deep spiritual awakening has come to our church. Attendance is up, giving is up, service is up, we have added a second full time pastor, bought up additional property."

All praise to our wonderful Lord!

Our plant is on US city route 30 into Lima, with thousands of vehicles passing every day. Many times I stand at my office window and look out at the flow of traffic, longing to be able to touch every one of those people with my witness.

So, when we built one of our new additions, the thought came to add a touch of witness. This we did with large stainless steel letters which spell out boldly, *Christ is the Answer.*

God has used that added dimension of witness again and again.

For instance, one day a redheaded salesman about forty years of age came into my office.

"I drove past your plant and saw that sign. What does it mean?"

"Just what it says," I told him. "Christ is the answer."

"Well," he said, "I belong to the Kiwanis Club over in Sidney and, when I saw that sign, I thought to myself that you might be a good speaker."

He invited me to address their Easter meeting.

Then the Holy Spirit touched my heart with a deep sense of this man's condition.

"By the way, sir," I said quietly, "do you perchance have a spiritual need?"

"I sure do," he said.

I closed the doors to my office.

"I'm a chain smoker," he began, "and with all the scare of cancer, I've tried to stop, but I can't. And besides that, I'm an alcoholic. As a salesman I have to entertain a lot, and I get to drinking and can't stop."

It was my privilege to point him to the transforming power of the gospel of Jesus Christ.

Several years ago, a member of the Inter-varsity organization came to my office and introduced me to a concept I had never considered before.

"All across America," he said, "people are developing prayer partnerships. A man with a man. A woman with a woman. They meet at least once a week and pray for each other.

"You know," he continued, "every Christian has weak spots in his life, the area where Satan attacks, but if two pray together, they share each others strength."

He pointed out that prayer partners are found all through the Bible. Moses had Aaron, David had Jonathan, Paul had Silas.

And, in more contemporary times, Charles Finney had Mr. Nash, and D. L. Moody had Ira D. Sankey.

If two of you shall agree on earth as touching anything that they shall ask, Jesus promised us, *it shall be done for them by my Father, who is in heaven.*[3]

God gave me such a prayer partner in Art, a fellow businessman in town.

For over ten years we have met every Thursday from noon till one o'clock in a remote park. There we pray for each other, our families, our businesses. But most of all we pray for the lost.

And one year we saw some forty decisions for Christ as a result of this prayer effort!

We have entered into a wide tract distribution ministry, serving laundromats in the area. A Christian radio station has been developed.

If you haven't already done so, I would urge you to develop such a prayer relationship.

Most of all, I urge you to keep growing, keep glowing, keep yielding yourself to the Holy Spirit as you reach out to the world around you. Look for new and better opportunities to make Christ known, always remembering the importance of the one-to-one relationship.

Be sane in your witness. As you experience success in reaching the lost, Satan will surely try to move in, to make you proud, or to turn you into some kind of fanatic. But, through daily cleansing by the Holy Spirit and careful study of the Bible, just stay yourself. People are drawn to someone with whom they can identify and, for a lost man, that someone needs to be a normal human being, not some kind of religious freak.

And widen your horizon by encouraging others. Don't try to pressure people into following your example. Graciously inspire them to follow your example!

"Lift your eyes, and look on the fields," Jesus challenges us, *"for they are white already to harvest."* [4]

Remember, somebody fulfilled God's plan in serving as the human instrument to bring you to Christ.

Now let the Holy Spirit use you as His instrument for reaching others!

[1] John 14:26.
[2] John 15:5.
[3] Matthew 18:19.

God has given me a wonderful staff of people to help run the business. They make it possible for me to manage our business without a constant five-days-a-week at my desk.

When we built our present corporation complex, I wanted to include a visual witness. "Christ Is the Answer" has been a blessing to many.

Now that the children are grown and gone, I'm home less than before. But I do set aside time to be with my dear wife Juanita.

These are solid silver bars, made from silver reclaimed in photographic processing rooms. We refine the reclaimed metal to form these valuable bars.

The Power of Faith

—WOODI ISHMAEL

"But thou shalt remember the Lord thy God: for it is he that giveth thee power to get wealth, that he may establish his covenant . . ." Deuteronomy 8:18.

I've found that tactful witness opens many doors—such as this cartoonist's visualization of our witness as a Christ-centered business.

May I Help You?

I'd like to think that, through the ministry of this book, I am now on your soul winning team!

If you have any questions, or anything you'd especially like to share, please let me hear from you.

Stanley Tam
US Plastics Corp.
1390 Neubrecht Rd.
Lima, Ohio 45801